Praise for *Wild Freedom:*
The Princess Who Found Her Name
On Fairy Tales, Imagination, and the Creative Mind

"Kushner's riveting fairy tale is a story of pilgrimage and re-enchantment, speaking simultaneously to the child and the reflective adult in us all. This beautifully layered book addresses the practical application of Jung's emphasis on the healing power of the imagination to grapple with irreconcilable opposites toward a new sense of wholeness."

-Miriam Stein PhD, Jungian Analyst

"Dreams and imagination are as much a part of the natural world as the stars that shine and the rain that falls. During a time of crisis and within an analytic process, a young writer bravely embarks on a journey of self-exploration by placing herself, uncharacteristically, at the center of a magical and unfolding story imbued with emotion and authentic truth. Present to both her own inner ecology and that of the larger surrounding world, she engages in active imagination and experiences herself anew and apart from the entrapment in a pathological family relational pattern. Surrounded by the transcendent power of "amazing grace," we see transformation within the tale penned by the younger self as well as in thoughtful reflections from the mature self. By stepping out of the family constellation and through a portal into the wilds of imagination, she comes to recognize endless possibilities in the never-ending Infinite."

-Linda Carter, MSN, Jungian Psychoanalyst

"Hauntingly beautiful poetic and true, is the fairy tale of "The Princess Who Found her Name" by Dale M. Kushner, and so sensitive and insightful the interpretation of the tale by three of the world's best Jungian Analysts! *Wild Freedom* is an eye opening read for sisters and brothers and parents and a guide to the soul's never-ending capacity to foster understanding and thus set us free—to come home to self."

-Kristina Schellinski, Author of *Individuation for Adult Replacement Children, Ways of Coming into Being*

WILD FREEDOM

The Princess Who Found Her Name

On Fairy Tales, Imagination, and the Creative Mind

By

Dale M. Kushner

CHIRON PUBLICATIONS • ASHEVILLE, NORTH CAROLINA

www.ChironPublications.com

Front cover illustration by Brooke Shaden
Interior artwork by Viviane Silvera, courtesy of the artist
Interior and cover design by Danijela Mijailovic
Printed primarily in the United States of America.

ISBN 978-1-68503-650-8 paperback
ISBN 978-1-68503-651-5 hardcover
ISBN 978-1-68503-652-2 electronic
ISBN 978-1-68503-653-9 limited edition paperback
ISBN 978-1-68503-654-6 limited edition hardcover

Library of Congress Cataloging-in-Publication Data Pending

Dedication

For my daughters, Jessie and Jennifer, wise teachers whose transformations are braided with my own.

To Judith Claire Mitchell, truest sister.
And for Burt: once upon a time and forever after.

In remembrance of Kevin "Mc" McIlvoy

She had a new feeling, the feeling of danger; on which a new remedy rose to meet it, the idea of an inner self or, in other words, of concealment.

Henry James, *What Maisie Knew*

All this was long ago, when I was still babyish and sure that everything was alive, not only the river or the rain, but chairs, looking-glasses, cups, saucers, everything.

Jean Rhys, *Wide Sargasso Sea*

Author's Note

In an enchanted world, everything is connected. Every *thing* speaks to every other thing. Such is the world of resonances. Invisible communication radiates between trees and the soil microbes that nourish them, between dragonflies and the lily pads on which they breed. In the country of the possible, rattlers and granite cliffs share a dream of sunlight's benevolence and lakes becalm under the moon's cool gaze. An encounter with the aliveness of this living, breathing, speaking non-human universe upends our notion of reality, of linear time, and of language as merely descriptive. For us writers, words and images create worlds.

But in a state of bereavement, perception shrinks. Vision dulls and turns inward. The vast surround of beauty and mystery goes unnoticed by the despairing soul. As you will soon read, so it was with me. Until...

The Littlest Princess came to my aid when I was disoriented and foundering. She arrived carrying a love letter from the Self that infused me with a fresh animating energy, a dervish wind that swept me out of a stupor, and not because I willed or predicted this would happen or even *made* it happen. I could not and did not foresee that I would be possessed by a fairy tale that flew from my pen onto the page in the silence of a sanctuary by a lake.

Nor could I have predicted that decades later, at the time of this writing, I would rediscover the Littlest Princess and be astonished at how her travails and mythic heroine's journey are still personally meaningful and archetypally relevant.

For the legendary writer Ursula K. Le Guin, our capacity to imagine, not our opposable thumbs, is humankind's most useful tool; she could imagine herself without thumbs but not without her imagination. "To train the mind to take off from immediate reality and return to it with new understanding and new strength, nothing equals poem and story," she says in her 2016 talk, "The Operating Instructions."

For all who enter the luminous darkness of this book, may the good fairies of patience, courage and curiosity abide with you, and may they whisper their unspoken stories in your ear.

Contents

Foreword

By Kenneth W. James

It is a genuine privilege to introduce this extraordinary volume, which offers readers a richly woven tapestry of narrative and insight in the form of *Wild Freedom: The Princess Who Found Her Name* alongside a constellation of compelling essays. This collection serves as both a landmark of imaginative storytelling and a profound exploration of the psychological and cultural dimensions that enrich the tale. Together, they invite readers into a transformative journey—one that transcends the boundaries of the page and resonates deeply with the universal quest for self-understanding and freedom.

It is not surprising that Kushner's story would give rise to a volume such as this. Kushner is a writer, a poet, and a scholar of Jung's thought. The capacity she has for deep reflection is demonstrated in the fairy tale itself, as well as in her essay, which describes how the story presented itself to and through her. Kushner's capacity to stand apart from her fairy tale allows the reader a rare glimpse into the writing process itself, setting the stage for three other reflective essays by Jungian analysts who each engaged with the tale in their own way. Kushner says in her essay in this volume, "Writing as Self-Enchantment," that writing the fairy tale released her from a bewitchment, breaking a spell. This revelation is significant because it validates a point Jung made in his essay "Psychology and Literature," which appears in Volume 15 of the *Collected Works*. In paragraph 159, he says, "It makes no difference whether the artist knows that (her) work is generated, grows, and matures within (her), or whether (she) imagines it is (her) own invention. In reality, it grows out of (her) as a child its mother. The creative process has a feminine quality, and the creative work arises from unconscious depths—we might truly say from the realm of the Mothers." Kushner's understanding of the origin and power of the fairy tale that came through her permits her to stand outside the tale itself and offer her reflections to the reader.

Kushner's fairy tale, the heart of this book, is a masterful creation, a narrative that is at once intimate, personal, and archetypal. It recounts the journey of a young princess ensnared within the shadows of familial envy and the yearning to please, who ultimately discovers a path to authentic selfhood marked by courage, transformation, healing, and reconciliation. This story's layers—its poetic language, magical motifs, and symbolism—offer a mirror to the reader's own inner life and the complexity of becoming whole in a confounding world fraught with challenges and mystery. Its timeless themes—identity, separation, and the reclamation of the true name—make it a story for all ages and times, holding both the mystery and the practicality of personal growth.

In her commentary on the fairy tale, Dale M. Kushner offers her deep reflection on the creative process itself as a form of self-enchantment and healing. Through her personal narrative, she reveals how the act of writing the tale emerged as a vital response to crisis and transformation, highlighting the power of imagination as a restorative force that connects us to the depths of the unconscious.

Kushner's voice is both vulnerable and inspiring, illuminating the origins of the story and its meaning as a beacon in turbulent times.

In reflecting on the tale, Murray Stein leads the reader through a thorough and accessible analysis rooted in Jungian thought. He artfully demonstrates how this fairy tale maps the archetypal journey of individuation—movement from the constraining social persona toward the liberating awareness of the Self. Stein's perspective encourages readers to consider how the motifs of separation, initiation, and reintegration echo timeless human experiences and psychological truths, deepening appreciation for the tale's universal significance.

Dariane Pictet's essay offers a richly symbolic and psychological reading, inviting readers to explore the profound inner processes represented in the princess's transformations and encounters. Her reflections emphasize the delicate balance and integration of opposing inner forces, highlighting the feminine journey toward embracing complexity and healing fractured parts of the self. Through her insights, the story unfolds as a map of the soul's movement toward wholeness and creative empowerment.

Henry Abramovitch brings a unique cultural and relational lens, focusing on the dynamics of sibling relationships, the meaning of naming, and the shadowy realms of envy and competition. His commentary situates the tale within a wider social and spiritual context, enriching the book with nuanced understandings of family identity and the psychological patterns that shape human connection. Abramovitch's exploration of spirituals and song as metaphorical and literal sources of resilience adds a vital note of hope and communal strength.

Together, the fairy tale and these essays form an integrated and multifaceted conversation. The collection is not merely a literary offering but a psychological and cultural resource. It challenges readers to confront the inherited "traps" of people-pleasing and self-betrayal, to recognize the roles played by family dynamics and inner conflict, and to find the courage to claim one's true name—a name that signifies multiplicity, freedom, and self-recognition. The tale's invitation to name the trap by its true name and the essays' exploration of this theme create a powerful through-line, making the volume both a work of art and a profound tool for introspection and growth.

In today's world, where many experience fragmentation, displacement, and pressure to conform, this book stands as a luminous guide. It reminds us that transformation is always possible and that the stories we tell ourselves—and each other—are vital keys to healing and becoming fully ourselves. Readers who engage with this work will find not only enchantment but also a practical and sensitive companion on their own journeys of individuation and renewal.

It is with heartfelt encouragement that I invite you to enter this remarkable book, to let the fairy tale's mystery and the essays' wisdom speak to you, and to discover through the story and reflections a richer, more expansive vision of identity, compassion, sacrifice, and freedom. May your reading be an enriching passage into the depths of imagination and self-understanding, leaving you inspired, challenged, and deeply connected to the enduring power of story.

Princess at Window

The Littlest Princess or The Princess Who Found Her Name

By Dale M. Kushner

I

The Littlest Princess

Once there lived a queen and her daughter, Princess N. The Queen loved her daughter, but she also envied her. She envied the princess her eyes, which had not yet seen sorrow; she envied the princess her laugh, which bubbled forth at the slightest merriment. She even envied the princess her sleep, which was the sleep of animals safe in their lair. But what the Queen envied most was the princess's life, which was just beginning to unfold.

The Queen was not old, but already she glimpsed Death behind her in the mirror when she rouged her cheeks. It was Death who whispered to the Queen that she should birth another child, Death being greedy for more souls to snatch. "Yes, yes," the Queen thought, "another child," and remembered how wonderfully alive she had felt during her pregnancy with Princess N.

Time passed and another princess was born. Now it was Princess N's turn to be envious. As the Queen bent to kiss her new baby, Princess N saw a smile lift her mother's lips. It was the very same smile that had been meant for only her. Princess N felt tears burn her eyes and her heart turn to steel. When the Littlest Princess gurgled and cooed, the Queen's smile grew even more radiant. "I too will make my mother smile," thought Princess N, and set about imitating the baby's strange and incomprehensible sounds. But the Queen was not pleased. "Don't be ridiculous. Act your age," she snapped, holding the precious infant to her breast and shoving Princess N out of her chamber.

"Precious-shmecious," huffed Princess N, and the eensy-weensy spark of love that had begun to grow for the Littlest Princess sputtered and went out. Princess N made a vow; she would make her sister's life miserable and drive the Littlest Princess away. Then she would again be her mother's favorite.

Princess N kept true to her vow. As her little sister grew, Princess N crept to her bed each night. In a voice gruff as an ogre's, she told her sister stories about red-eyed monsters, witches, and murderers. Frightened, the Littlest Princess would cry out in her sleep. At first the Queen rushed to comfort her, but when the Littlest Princess's nightmares continued, encouraged by Princess N's nightly tales, the Queen grew angry at having her sleep disturbed. "What a foolish imagination you have," she complained, and plugged her ears when the Littlest Princess called to be comforted. "I am succeeding," thought Princess N gleefully, and pinched and poked her baby sister in the darkness. And this was how the Littlest Princess learned to bite her tongue to keep from crying, and to sniff up all her tears.

On those nights when the Littlest Princess could not sleep—for sleep meant falling into a pit crowded with demons—she rose from her bed to gaze out the window where the moon balanced delicately above the highest mountain. "Moon-Maiden, Moon-Maiden," she sang, "How far away you are. Moon-Maiden, Moon-Maiden, come for me now." Long into the night, the Littlest Princess would sing her song until the birds stirring among the silver leaves added their voices to hers. The Moon-Maiden, however, never answered and gave no sign she heard the Littlest Princess.

Princess N continued to tease and torment the Littlest Princess, sometimes leading her to an unfamiliar part of the royal gardens before disappearing without warning. Sometimes she challenged her sister to climb the ancient fruit trees that stood in the orchard. "Bet you can't, bet you can't," taunted Princess N, until the Littlest Princess, who took some pride in her climbing skills, scrambled up a gnarled trunk. "Higher, higher. Higher still," encouraged the voice from the ground, and the Littlest Princess would climb higher until she was straddling the topmost branch which was about crack under her weight.

The Littlest Princess grew more and more confused. It was unthinkable that her older sister did not love her, and so she did not let herself think it. Instead, another thought popped into her head: *My sister, Princess N, is displeased with me. I must be displeasing. I must try harder to please her.*

That is how the Littlest Princess became known to some in the royal household as Princess Please-Her.

Meanwhile, the Queen was growing old and fat. Death wiggled in next to her when she made her toilette, his bony finger smudging crimson over her lips, glittery blue powder on her eyelids. "Lovely, lovely," he purred. Being vain and ignorant, the Queen grew bewitched by Death who was all the while cleverly composing her death mask.

One afternoon, noticing how quickly the purple grapes turned soft and rotten, the Queen had a startling thought. If her daughters, the princesses, should die, she would be alone in the royal household. The Queen shuddered. "I must prevent the princesses from ever leaving me and keep them out of Death's clutches."

Long into midnight hours, the Queen tossed and turned and listened for the daughters' slightest moan, ready to again jump into action if one of them called. But Princess N slept like a drunken dwarf, and the Littlest Princess had already learned the high art of silencing her terror. "I shall watch over the princesses day and night, night and day," thought the Queen, and so commanded her servants to keep a log of everywhere the princesses went. Never were they to climb the fruit trees in the garden or swim in the icy black river that wove through the palace grounds, and never were they to wander beyond the palace walls.

Soon the Queen grew bored with her vigil. "Why should I waste my time," she thought one fine morning, "when the princesses are perfectly safe inside the palace walls where no one and nothing can harm them," and with a self-satisfied smile, she nodded at her reflection three times in the mirror.

Winter arrived as it always did. The wind blew and snow glistened on the bare branches. The Queen felt time passing in her bones. She saw that her daughters' feet had grown two sizes larger. To her dismay, the Queen's hair was now sprinkled with gray. One night, the Littlest Princess heard her mother the Queen scolding Time itself. "Who do you think you are, measuring out my minutes and hours when I have commanded you to slow down?" But Time only laughed in her face and continued to tap out her heartbeat minute by minute, year by year. Time angered the Littlest Princess's mother. The frosty North wind angered her. The crow at her window angered her. Everything angered the Queen, including the Littlest Princess herself. Seeing that there was nothing and no one to make her mother happy, the Littlest Princess swore to take on the job to Please-Her Highness the Queen and Please-Her Highness Princess N. In one pocket she carried all the compliments she could possibly scribble on a scrap of paper, and in the other pocket she carried a list of services and noble actions she would perform.

One year, two years, three years went by, and the Littlest Princess could think of nothing else but how to stay in her family's good graces. She hadn't the time to think about the other things she longed to do, like follow the bees to their hive and steal some golden honey or climb into the pear tree and sing with the finchbirds, or build herself a little hut at the edge of the garden where she could sleep under the stars. Every so often, a voice would tell her to say NO! to her mother and sister and for a moment she would feel wildly free. "Yes, I long to be free," she would say to herself, "but if I refuse my mother and my sister, they will stamp their feet and pull their hair. My mother, the Queen, will pound her chest and accuse me of breaking her heart. Perhaps she would turn me out of the household forever."

The princess thought about this. "Isn't that exactly what I want? If only I knew how to live in the outside world." Then a terrifying fear would swoop down on her. "If I leave, I will be lost. What will I eat? Where will I sleep? How will I protect myself?" In her most private self, the Littlest Princess wondered if she was good for anything except being a Please-Her. She began to wish that she could become invisible. Once again she beseeched the Moon-Maiden for help, but the Moon-Maiden remained mute. Nonetheless, beautiful melodies that comforted her flowed from the Littlest Princess's throat and lightened her sorrow.

Silent Moon-Maiden

One evening, when the pear trees in the garden showed their frilly blossoms and the pussy willows wore their spring fur, as the Littlest Princess perched on her window seat ready to sing to the Moon-Maiden, she noticed a shadow sliding over the white pebbles on the path below. The shadow moved like a breeze over water, vanishing before the princess could even open her mouth. "Perhaps it is only the night-faces of the roses nodding to each other under the moonlight," she thought. "Or the willow saplings, dipping to kiss the edge of the river." The Littlest Princess leaned further out her window. The moon shone like the inside of an oyster shell. "I must be imagining it," she sighed. "There is no one among the irises and roses. The night is as lonely as I." But just as she said those very words, two yellow eyes winked up at her from the darkness, and before she could string together another sentence, the shadow was strutting across her windowsill in the form of a mink.

"Be careful what you wish for," said the mink, balancing on his back legs and looking the Littlest Princess straight in eye. Startled, the Littlest Princess replied, "Whatever do you mean?" Before answering, the mink scrubbed his face with his tiny paws. Despite his size, the mink's voice was rough and commanding and reminded the Littlest Princess of the wheels of the royal carriage grinding over the gravel roads.

"I heard what you wished for, sister," said the mink, staring at her with great seriousness. "You wished to be invisible. You wished to be free." "True,

true," confessed the princess, adding somewhat apologetically, "the life of a princess is not what it would seem." The mink waited for her to continue. "I am miserable," she admitted. "I am never at peace. I cannot please the Royal Highnesses the Queen and Princess N. These days when the Queen looks at me, tears sprout under her lashes. Sometimes she touches my cheek and just when I think she is about to bestow a kiss or praise the fine work I've done with the mending and gardening, she cries out as if lanced by a sword—*Youth flies quickly by. Once I was young and beautiful like you*—and seeing only the lost parts of herself in me, she turns away to sob in earnest. Pity drives me to tell her that her beauty is everlasting, but if I should lie in this way, as if by some perversion, a new crease appears on my mother's cheek." The Littlest Princess took a deep breath. The mink nodded for her to continue.

"As for my sister, Princess N, another form of envy breeds in her, for she has youth and beauty and riches as well. Yet her mission is to ruin my happiness and taint it with her misery. It is not the hard household work I mind," concluded the Littlest Princess, "for that alone might bring a rightful satisfaction. But labor for the wrong reasons is empty of joy."

The Littlest Princess had not finished before the mink, who had been an arm's distance away, hopped onto her shoulder. "Envy," he said. "That's a tough one. I'll tell you, sister, you've got your work cut out for you." He dabbed her teardrops with the bush of his tail.

In a voice silky as milkweed, the Littlest Princess continued. "I wish—I wish to be like you," she said to the mink. "Free to dance with the night shadows. Free to let the river carry me out beyond the palace gates. These wishes I ask the Moon-Maiden to grant." The Littlest Princess's eyes filmed over as she spoke. For a moment, her body was transported up into the heavenly spheres where the Moon-Maiden rested in her mantle of navy clouds. Seeing how the Littlest Princess had begun to drift into the vaporous reaches, the mink tapped his sharp claws on her neck.

"Tsk, tsk," he snorted. "Wishes and dreams, dreams and wishes. Call to the Moon-Maiden if you like, but this here mink catches the fishes!" With this he did a little pirouette and smiled a sly smile. Annoyed, the Littlest Princess was preparing to say "Scat," for it seemed to her that the mink was making nonsense of her troubles, but the mink grew serious once again.

"They see you for what you are not," he said solemnly, "and not for what you are. To please is to lie, a trap you lie in." The mink stamped his feet in a lively jig on the Littlest Princess's shoulder. Tucking a strand of hair behind her ear, he confided, "The trap was set before you were born. The trap will exist after you die. Name the trap by its true name, and you will be free."

The mink's words echoed in her ear. Turning her head, the princess was about to ask the mink a question when she found he had suddenly disappeared. She repeated his words aloud. She had been given the instructions: *Name the trap, and you will be free*. Whatever did that mean? She must find a way to understand the mink's riddle.

As if by habit, the Littlest Princess gazed up at the moon, which had floated free of its hazy yoke. It hung above the darkened landscape, a golden door, waiting to be opened.

II
Princess-Mink

The Littlest Princess awoke to the sun's rays climbing up the windowpanes. During the night, the world had been totally transformed. The fine oak armoire that stood in a corner of the room now appeared gigantic, rising to ceiling height. Her bed was a vast prairie of blankets and pillows in which she could easily get lost. When she looked around, she saw all movement at once: the spider embroidering a new web above the lintel, and dust motes dancing in a slant of sunlight. "What has happened?" wondered the Littlest Princess. And in less time than it takes to swallow a breath, she knew. She looked down at her body. It was covered with a fine chestnut fur. She had whiskers. Paws. The princess had become a mink.

She did not hesitate. Swiftly to the window and down the stone-faced palace wall, the Princess-Mink fled into the garden. As she clamored over the wide lawn, sunlight warmed her body, stoking her with new energy. "How good this feels," exclaimed Princess-Mink, "how delicious freedom is," and she made a silent vow to thank the mink who surely was responsible for her deliverance.

Over the groomed palace lawns sped the Princess-Mink. Her eyes, which she realized were ever so much keener, accomplished a wide and detailed circle of sight. Each blade of grass was a green obelisk strung with beads of water within whose spheres a myriad of forms jiggled and spun. "It's all too beautiful," cried the Princess-Mink, and her new lithe body shook with heartfelt laughter. "This is freedom, I'm sure."

But just as that thought sprang into her mind, her sharp eyes caught sight of two large figures striding over a distance hill. Their shadows bounded forward at an alarming pace. She felt a cold knot under her ribcage spreading to the tips of her ears. The sun itself had vanished, and the sky lay over her, heavy and gray.

"Mink?" a voice exclaimed.

"Mink! Mink!!" chimed the other. "A cape for my lady."

"A blanket for my baby."

"Boots for the snow."

"A fine cap to show."

Panic spread through Princess-Mink's body as she listened to the uses the hunters imagined for her pelt.

"A beauty," she heard one say.

"Yes, a beauty," came the answer. "She's mine. I saw her first." The men began to argue. "No, no," Princess-Mink wanted to yell. "It's me, the Littlest Princess!," but alas, she could not make herself understood.

A loud crack bit into the air. From the corner of her eye, the Princess-Mink caught the sheen of their guns and smelled the acrid odor of human sweat and gunpowder staining the air. In desperation, she headed for the river. Upon reaching its banks, though the princess had never once been allowed to swim in the river, she leapt in without a thought. Down down down she dove, slipping inside the frigid current. Soon the gunshots grew fainter and fainter. When she was sure the hunters had been left far behind, the Princess-Mink rose to the surface, swiveled onto her back and let the current take her where it was headed.

For days, the Princess-Mink drifted on the river, buoyant as a petal. Above her, the trees made a roof of a hundred shades of green. From the crown of a cottonwood, a black-hooded raven cawed his hello. Small dust-colored birds added their cheery notes, hip-hopping from branch to branch. "This is all so peaceful," thought the Princess-Mink. Occasionally, a brazen hawk swooped menacingly close. The princess hid among the reeds until the predator had captured an unlucky rabbit instead.

It was on one of these days that Princess-Mink became aware of a thought worrying her as surely as a thorn in her paw. She had not forgotten the mink's words—*Name the trap by its true name, and you will be free*. But though she had not named the trap, now she felt as free as free can be. "A puzzling puzzle," she thought. "I have left my mother the Queen and my sister Princess N far behind, am I not free?" The very next morning she woke up with these words from a dream in her head. *Freedom is merely your guide. Pay attention to where it takes you.* "I'm tired of riddles," said the Princess-Mink sulkily. "All the rivers and forests and meadows are now my domain. I must indeed be free."

In the way that streams lead to rivers and rivers to the sea, one day the Princess-Mink realized the river in which she had been swimming had changed. It no longer smelled of iron and had turned sluggish and thickly green. She dipped her tongue into the water, recoiling at its brackish taste. She had entered a swamp. "How far I have come," thought the Princess-Mink.

Over the next days, the Princess-Mink discovered new delights: birds bright as butterflies, schools of iridescent fish that surrounded her like a garland of angels before disappearing into underwater meadows. She watched the silly side-scuttling crabs and delighted in the juicy purple fruits that fell from the trees. "Surely this is freedom," she said to herself. "I think I will stay right here forever."

Night dropped flawlessly. A thousand tinny stars poked holes in the black mat of heaven. One evening, when the Princess-Mink was just beginning to feel a tug of loneliness, she shivered as she watched the moon rise above the farthest corner of the earth, its twin horns glowing ivory. Not in many, many weeks had she sung to the Moon-Maiden. "Moon-Maiden, Moon-Maiden," she began and then she stopped: she could not remember what she needed to ask the moon. The night's darkness surrounded her, wrapping her in its silence. There are many types of silences, she said to herself, the silence before a storm when the earth readies itself in stillness; the silence of deer hidden in a stand of birch. But the silence of the human heart is the most terrible silence of all. That's when Death waits nearby with his woolly sack.

Princess-Mink felt loneliness enter her like a ghost entering an empty house. All the other creatures of the earth and sky and water had disappeared. Only the percussive beat of her own heart threaded its way through the darkness. Princess-Mink fell asleep knowing she must move on. "As lovely as this place is," she thought, "I am a stranger here. It is not my home."

The next morning Princess-Mink paddled out of the swamp. After an hour or so, the brackish water became a trickle that ended at a wide sand beach. Beyond the beach was water, more water than the Princess-Mink had ever seen. "It falls off the edges of the earth," Princess-Mink said in wonderment. "The sea, the sea!," she shouted. "At last I have come to the sea," and immediately launched herself into the sparkling swells.

In she went, and out she rolled, coughing up salt water that stung her eyes and nose. Determined, the Princess-Mink tried again, as fast has her little legs could carry her, but the sea spit her out and threw her, dazed, onto the sand. A flotilla of pink crabs trekked halfway across the beach before being swept away by the tide's sleight-of-hand. Her own predicament was equally as dismal. She could not go forward, since she was not built to swim in the sea and would never go backward to retrace her journey. "For what?" she thought, "To find myself back at the palace?" That, too, was unthinkable. "How to cross the sea is not a problem a mink can easily solve," she thought. The mink who had given her his shape was no longer useful to her. In her heart she thanked him for the great gift he had bestowed and wondered what to do next.

Princess Contemplating the Sea

III.
Bird-Girl

Princess-Mink waited for a solution to pop into her head, but she could not sit still. The sea showed her its many faces—angry, turbulent, serene—but she was not amused. Hauling herself back and forth across the beach, she grew very tired, and finding no answer about what to do next, she decided to do nothing and see what the morning would bring.

Just as she was about to close her eyes something shifted across her pupils some distance away. Straining to see what it was, she caught sight of a slight movement at the periphery of her vision. It resembled a silver blue umbrella stuck in the sand. “It can’t be,” she thought, a giggle bubbling up inside her. Amused by the unusual sight, for a moment the heavy stone over her heart lifted.

Stumbling to her feet, the Princess-Mink scampered down the beach, slowing to catch her breath as she neared the strange object. When she was several yards away, she saw that it was not an umbrella at all, but a tall slender bird. Balancing on one leg, the bird was thin as a pole, its head tucked under a wing. His cobalt eye was watching her.

Seeing the princess approach, the bird popped his head out from the spray of feathers and set down his other spindly leg. He shook himself out, then stood knock-kneed, head thrust forward, staring at Princess-Mink with piercing eyes. Princess-Mink was too stupefied to be frightened. With great dignity, the bird bowed. Thrusting out his chest in an operatic gesture, he began to sing. *River of Jordan is chilly and co-oo-old, chills the body, but not the so-ou-l.* The Princess-Mink stood mesmerized.

The bird flew low over the ground to where Princess-Mink gawked, amazed. Landing at her feet, he swung his long neck down to her level. "Come to the end of it, have you?" His voice came out hoarse and breathless having squeezed its way up the lengthy pipeline of his neck. "Oh yes, sooner or later, we all reach the sea," he said knowingly. And with great bearing continued:

River of Jordan is chilly and wi-ii-de
Milk and honey on the other si-ii-de.

"And now you've got to figure out where to go from here, isn't that right? In it, over it, through it. You pick your number, and you take your chances." He looked her up and down. *Michael row your boat ashore...*

"Now it just so happens this very morning, I am heading out across this hazy dazy lazy lap of water. Heading out to the Isle of What. Be glad to take you with me, Mz Mink. I'm your man if you're wanting to go that way. Think on it a few minutes." The bird scurried off into some low-lying scrub to let Princess-Mink worry out her answer in private.

Princess-Mink sat in the sand and argued with herself. "What a loony bird. Should I trust him? What choice do I have? Maybe I should swim back up the river? And return to the palace?" The thought revolted her. "Maybe I could live somewhere along the way, somewhere between here and there? But would it be, could it be home? Maybe I could stay, here and live by the sea?" But then she remembered her loneliness, vast as the sea itself. "Confusion, confusion," thought Princess-Mink, watching the creature at a tidal pool, preening his pin feathers. Seeing that he might provide amusing company, she yelled, "I'm coming with you, Bird."

"Hallelujah!" said the bird. "Praise the Lord. You won't regret it, Mz Mink. I promise you. Climb on, my friend, and hold on tight."

As instructed, the Princess-Mink stretched her body over the bird's back. Beneath his bones she felt the sturdy engine of his heart. Her own heart felt as if it had legs and was cantering uphill. As they rose into the sky, the world fell away into a jigsaw puzzle of blues and greens. Up and up they soared, the taste of wind in her mouth.

"Howdy-do. Name's Hieronymous," the bird said as they swept through the belly of a cloud.

Hieronymous, the Princess-Mink decided, was a sleek machine. Awkward on land, he flew effortlessly through the air. In a few minutes, her body relaxed. She had to admit, she was enjoying herself. The sea shone below and the sky above.

After a while, Hieronymous encouraged her to test her flying skills. "If you want to fly, you got to pump them arms. One, two, three—glide. One, two, three—glide. Like dancing. Let go of me and give her a try."

Princess-Mink was afraid, but she let the bird's wings guide her. One, two, three—glide. One, two, three—glide. Soon she felt lighter than a cloud and happier than the happiest time she could remember. "Oh surely this must be freedom," thought the Princess-Mink, whose joy at that moment was as boundless as the sky. "I did not know there is a bird alive inside me." No sooner had she thought those words than her mink pelt transformed into satiny white feathers.

For many days the two followed the sun in its westward arc across the sky. Hieronymous sang hymns and gospel and country songs from his repertoire. "Singing practically keeps me alive when I'm doing a solo," he told her. "I will teach you the words, if you like. I will also teach you how to sleep on the wing, how to fish like an expert, how to milk clouds for a little fresh water—the essentials," he said, and did as he promised, with great patience and gentlemanly generosity. On the fifth day of their journey, on a morning when the sea and the sky were enameled a perfect blue, the Bird-Girl noticed something golden bobbing in the waters below. Hieronymous had flown ahead, and Bird-Girl called to him, as she thought she heard a voice coming from the golden orb.

"Hieronymous," she yelled. "Hieronymous, there is something in the sea that is calling to us."

The bird returned to her side. "Nonsense," said he. "It is only the sun reflecting on a bed of weeds. I've seen it a hundred times. The sun and the sea play tricks together. It's nothing, I tell you. Nothing at all."

Not satisfied, her heart leading her in another direction, the Bird-Girl circled back toward the mysterious object, which she saw now was not a golden orb at all, but the head of a boy whose pale hair caught and held the sunlight. The boy's face was the picture of consternation. She flew closer. He was trying to talk, but each time he opened his mouth, sea water poured in, and he sputtered. The Bird-Girl's heart filled with pity. She remembered the awkwardness of her minkself in the sea. She circled still lower until she was almost directly above the head and was able to hear his words:

"Been torn apart. Arms, legs, torso, all lost at sea. Help me. Help me please. Find all my pieces. Bring them back to me so I can be whole again."

Hieronymous had seen the Bird-Girl turn around. Now he retraced his trajectory and hovered by her side. The Princess-Mink could see that though her friend's spirit was buoyant, his body was tired, so she was not surprised when Hieronymous told her she would have to take on the boy's request by herself.

The Bird-Girl understood. "I wish I'd never come upon the poor boy's head," she admitted. "But since I have, I cannot forget it."

The boy's head implored, "Don't forget me. You can't forget me!"

Hieronymous looked at the Bird-Girl, his kind eyes brimming with concern for he knew what she was about to undertake alone. *It's a-me, it's a-me, it's a-me oh Lord, standing in the need of prayer*. The bird sang low and deep, the melody spilling from his mouth and surrounding all three of them in an aura of reverence. The Bird-Girl sighed. And even the head quieted down.

The Bird-Girl said, "I must have become a bird for some reason other than to fly myself across the sea. Perhaps it was to retrieve this boy's body?" To

Hieronymous she added, "You came to my rescue. If not for you, I should be a lost and lonely mink. You taught me to fly. You taught me..." And because she could not find the words to express all the gratitude she felt toward the bird, she cuffed him gently with her wing and planted a chaste kiss on his brow. The old bird shook the tears from his eyes, which fell drop by drop into the sea.

"Though you have learned how to fly, you are not a true bird, and though you have made the sky your home, you are not home. Do what you must. May you not falter on your mission." He bowed and headed off in the direction of the horizon.

As Hieronymous shrunk to a gray dot in the cloudless sky, the Bird-Girl sang one of his favorite songs: *Good news, chariot's a-coming, Good news, chariot's a-coming... And I don't want it to leave me behind.*

IV

The Head, The Body, The Arms and Legs

The sea began to churn. It slashed the air like a thousand pirate swords. The Bird-Girl fought against the strong updrafts. She had not a moment to feel the anguish over Hieronymous's departure before the head, bobbing in the rough sea called to her.

"Find my torso first. Bring it back with my heart intact," he commanded.

Seeing how the head struggled to keep afloat, the Bird-Girl understood the importance of the boy's body. "Surely a head needs a body, for what good is a head without all the other parts?" she thought and asked the head where to look first.

"How should I know?" the head answered rudely. "I have enough to do just to keep from drowning." He spit out a stream of water.

"Yes, yes, of course," said the Bird-Girl, feeling somewhat foolish. "Of course you have enough to do just to keep from drowning." And tired as she was the Bird-Girl spread her wings and climbed into the brilliant sky.

Hieronymous's memory kept her company as she gained altitude. His rich tenor reverberated in her head. She sang along: *River of Jordan is chilly and cold. Chills the body, but not the soul-ol.* It was while she was singing and trying not to miss any sign of the boy's body, that the Bird-Girl devised a plan. She knew that even with the best sense of direction, the sea was immense, and she could easily get lost. If the stars stayed hidden, and the moon slept in its other house, and the wind held its breath, she would have no way to know her bearings. Hieronymous had shown her the grid of invisible energy lines that cross-hatched the earth. She would search square by square over the surface of the entire sea until she found what the boy requested.

The Bird-Girl traveled far. Her wings ached. Her eyes burned. She longed for a pond in which to refresh herself: it was time to rest. A few stars salted the heavens. The sea shone purple in the changing light. The Bird-Girl descended low over the roiling sea. Once again, Hieronymous's presence surrounded her, and she felt comforted.

"And good night to you too, dear friend," she whispered. "Good night and thank you with all my heart." Having said this, the Bird-Girl alighted on a narrow missile of wood that would serve as a bed for the night.

In the morning, she awoke to a thumping against the side of her plank. Peering into the water, left and right, she saw the boy's water-logged body, blue-white as mother's milk. "What luck," said the Bird-Girl, her mind already charting the trip back to the head with her precious cargo.

For hours, under a hot sun, the Bird-Girl heaved and pulled, struggling to hoist the boy's body onto her narrow platform. "This is no job for a bird," she thought. "Perhaps I have made a mistake." But when she remembered the boy's eyes full of fear and hope, she resumed her task. After a long while of pushing and tugging, the Bird-Girl successfully dragged the boy's body onto the wooden plank. As it lay before her in the bright sunshine, she noticed a puckered slash across its chest above the place where his heart should have been. Sticking her feathered wingtip into the wound, she discovered the boy's heart had been removed.

"I have never seen anything as horrible as this disowned body," she said. She could not keep her eyes from the sad, empty pocket where the boy's heart had been. She remembered the command—the body was to be brought back with its heart intact. And now what was she to do? "I am only one small bird," she said to herself. "The sea extends farther than all the days and nights I have ever flown. I am tired, but perhaps it is still better to bring a body without a heart, than no body at all." In the next minute, she began to prepare for her flight.

The Bird-Girl labored under the weight of the boy's body, which she had fastened to her back with ropes of seaweed. Unbalanced, she tipped and pitched in the air like a drunken lout. It was twilight when the head saw her coming. "My body," he yelled. "You've found my body. Throw it down to me, Bird-Girl."

Despite her baggage, the Bird-Girl landed gracefully among the swells. Untying the body from her back, she shoved it in the direction of the head. The boy saw instantly what was missing.

"Birdbrain," he shouted. "Incompetent. Lily-livered. No-Good-Bird. Where is my heart?" His face was the color of beet juice; his golden hair had become spokes of flame.

"Missing," replied the Bird-Girl, for that was the truth.

"I know it's missing, you frowsy-feathered idiot. Without my heart, I'm no better than a speck of flotsam adrift on the sea. You must find my heart."

The Bird-Girl had only temporarily forgotten her own desire to find herself a home. Now she was assaulted by an intense longing. "On the one side," she reasoned, "I am trying to continue my passage across the sea. On the other side, the boy needs his heart and his arms and legs."

The boy sensed her hesitation. "Please. You're my last chance. Who knows who else will fly by. I have only this one request, and then you will be free to do as you like. Please bring back my arms and my legs and my heart."

The Bird-Girl had already decided. She said: "I will spend the next night and day in search of your lost parts, but if by the end of that time, I am unsuccessful, I shall be on my way."

"Okay, okay," said the head. "But please, hurry."

The sea swallowed the sun in a few quick gulps. A dense, suffocating darkness fanned out in all directions. The stars shrunk back into their holes. The Bird-Girl was afraid.

"What an impossible task this is," she said to herself. But dispirited as she was, she headed into the gloom, focusing all her attention on finding the butchered heart. Water and sky had become a common field of darkness. "Perhaps I am the only creature alive on the planet, except for the head," she said. "In that case, I shall sing." She broke out into a loud chorus of another of Hieronymous's favorite songs: *Am-aazing Grace, how sweet thy name*. "I wonder if this is freedom too," she said.

Past midnight, after the Bird-Girl had been sparring with a bitter wind for many hours, blurry-eyed and muscle-weary, she glimpsed in the distance, something opaline flickering under the sea. The sight rallied her energy, and she flew lower to get a better view. Hundreds of fish, each no larger than a child's finger and radiating a pale green phosphorescence wove a shimmering figure-eight a few feet below the water's surface. Swaying in the gentle cradle of the sea, they held their position as the Bird-Girl drew closer. When she was directly above them, they realigned, forming an arrow like those painted on an airfield.

Following the direction of the arrowhead, the Bird-Girl came at last to the boy's arms and legs bumping and jostling each other among the troughs. The Bird-Girl gave out a sigh of relief. "Now, I have only to find the heart," she said. She was about to thank the fish for their help, when she realized they had extinguished their lights and vanished into the depths.

The boy's limbs were slick and slippery, and each time the Bird-Girl attempted to fasten them to her back, they slid off like greased rolling pins. She worked for several hours without success before the idea came to her that she could bind the legs together to form a raft and use the arms as oars. In this way, she could row her way back to the boy.

The sky was mottled with the pale yellow of dawn before the Bird-Girl finished binding the legs and was set to begin her voyage. Roused from its nightly resting place, the sun rose slowly over a calm sea. The Bird-Girl imagined she saw Hieronymous circling overhead, but it was only an illusion sprung out of a prism of sea water that clung to her lashes.

The day was peaceful and the raft sailed easily aided by a gentle wind. The Bird-Girl thought how pleased the boy would be at the sight of his arms and his legs. "Now if only I could find his heart, all will be well, and I will be free to find a home." Just as those words came into her mind, the raft smacked loudly against a huge scaly wall that had materialized out of nowhere. It appeared to be the side of a very large fish. The fish righted itself in the water, and the raft with the Bird-Girl on it slipped onto its back. Round and round the fish swam, the Bird-Girl clutching its dorsal fin, the raft of legs rolling under her as if on ball-bearings. Without warning, the fish plunged underwater, and the raft came to rest at once in its wake. A second later, the creature broke surface and rose, rocket-like, in front of the Bird-Girl. The fish had a long, sharp sword-shaped nose which he now used to spear the Bird-Girl's chest, holding her aloft as he addressed her.

"You say something about a heart? You talking about a *gen-u-ine* boy's heart?"

The Bird-Girl stared into the slits of the fish's gunmetal eyes. They shone with a malevolent gleam. The fish had skewered her like a piece of meat. Pain ripped through her chest. "I am in the presence of powerful evil," she thought, "Neither the mink nor Hieronymous have taught me how to be cleverer than evil. I must find my own way."

Not to be hurried, the Bird-Girl cleared her throat and watched as the raft of the boy's arms and legs rocked gently in nearby swells.

"A boy's heart is missing," she said directly. "It has been stolen right out from his body. If you are the thief or can lead me to the thief, I will consider you a hero. And if you betray me, I will tell all the birds of the sea who eat your kind that you are a liar and a cheat, and they will find a way to punish you, and you will be no one's hero."

The fish gave a nasty laugh. "Who cares about that! In these parts, I am more feared and mightier than any do-gooder hero, I'm the most frightening fella around." He lowered his long rapier nose, and the Bird-Girl slid off into the water. By some miracle, she had not been greatly harmed.

"What'll you give me if I lead you to the heart?" demanded the fish.

The Bird-Girl stared into the fish's cruel eyes. She knew he was quite capable of tricking her, but at that very moment, she heard Hieronymous singing, *The river Jordan is chilly and cold, chills the body but not the soul*, and she thought, "Is it possible this braggard also has a soul?"

"I'll give you all my beautiful plumage, but only after you show me where I can find the boy's heart."

"Ah," said the fish, thinking only of his booty, "with feathers I will rule both sea and sky." His lips pulled back in a horrifying grin. "Done. Follow me."

V
Whose Heart?

Again, the fish led her far below where no light entered. The Bird-Girl tried to make conversation, but friendship was not the fish's business. "We made a deal," he said. "I lead you to the heart. You give me your feathers. That don't mean I gotta talk to you."

The Bird-Girl followed the fish down steep ravines, through canyons, over coral beds into a darkness so complete, she could barely make out a glimmer of his tail. When they reached their destination, the fish rested on the sea's floor. The Bird-Girl looked around. "In there," said the fish, pointing with his sword-snout to the mouth of a cave illuminated by a faint pink light.

The Bird-Girl nodded and handed over her feathered skin. This the fish lanced with his nose. Neither saying good-bye nor thanking her, the fish shot away.

A few feet in front of the Bird-Girl, illumined by the palest light, the mouth of a cave beckoned. She had never felt so alone. Nonetheless, she strode forward, a girl without fur or feathers once again.

The cave led through a series of pitch-black tunnels. Following the flickering light, she came to a large antechamber that was suffused in warm rosy glow. At the far end of the chamber was a heavy wooden door from behind which the light emanated. Pushing it open, the first thing she saw was a throne carved out of sea minerals and crystals. On the throne sat the figure of a deep-sea diver, its head, a metal bubble with a small glass aperture, its body, a metal suit. She saw no face behind the mask. From within the helmet a voice said, "You have come for the heart, no doubt?"

"Yes," she answered. "The boy's heart."

"Take it," said the voice wearily, "it doesn't fit," barking out his words like a small, irritated dog. "None of them fit." His arm made a sweeping motion to include an entire wall of shelves on which sat row after row of jars filled with human hearts.

VI
The Diver's Story

"Once upon a time, I may have been a man or a woman. Who knows? I can't remember," said the diver. "I do remember I arrived at the sea in search of something lost in its depths. I remember a boat and endless falling. When I reached the bottom, I was no longer human, and neither was I fish nor mollusk, octopus, nor stingray. I had become an intelligence without a body, and have been hiding in this metal shell since that fateful fall."

The Bird-Girl felt pity. She thought, "I am like the diver. No longer a mink or a bird and perhaps not even proper girl. What am I and where is my home?"

"And the hearts?" she asked the diver.

"I thought if I had a heart..."

The Bird-Girl smiled. She had heard this story before, about a metal man looking for a heart, but that was a different tale.

"It's no good. I can't get a heart inside this metal trap," said the diver.

The Bird-Girl wondered how many others beside the head and the diver were looking for hearts. She sighed. For a single second she was tempted to stay and help the diver, but she quickly realized the diver's dilemma was not hers to solve. The boy was waiting.

"Shame on you for stealing other people's hearts," said the Bird-Girl. "That is not the way to get your own heart."

The diver replied, "Tell me a better way."

The girl closed her eyes and thought and thought. She remembered how Hieronymous had told her she could fly and taught her how, and so she did, but she did not know the proper lessons on how to make a heart appear. It was, she thought, a mystery.

"I came for the boy's heart, and if you will please give it to me now, I should like to leave," she said.

The diver pointed again to the wall of shelves, to the last jar on the highest board. Before the Bird-Girl could reach for it, the diver said, "It could happen to you, you know. It could happen to anyone. Losing your heart. And what would you have done?"

The Bird-Girl was not interested in the diver's excuses. As she reached on tippy toes for the jar holding the boy's heart, the jar leapt into her hands. Hugging it to her chest, she was zoomed upward by a terrific force and transformed back into her full human self.

VII
The Return

The journey back to the boy was almost instantaneous. The girl rose rapidly through the fathoms and found the raft waiting for her in the exact place she had left it. She jumped aboard, and with the help of the boy's arms, which rowed with the force of a hundred sturdy Vikings, she reached the boy's head in no time at all. His arms, legs, body and heart, recognizing their missing head, jumped into the sea to reassemble themselves, and the heart itself nestled into its old home.

When he was wholly composed once again, the boy addressed the girl with compassion. "And where will you go now?" he asked.

The girl was touched by his kindness. She had become accustomed to his brusque manner and desperate commands. "I will try to make my way across the sea," she said, "but since I no longer have wings to fly, or special lungs or gills and fins with which to swim, it will be a very slow journey."

The boy and the girl lay on their backs, floating. The boy nodded, his golden hair spilling out in a halo of light. The two were very quiet.

"Let us stay together a little longer," said the boy. "Whilst one of us swims, the other can sleep on the swimmer's back. When we reach the nearest shore, we can part ways and say good-bye."

The girl was agreeable and so they began their journey following the sun across the sky.

Amazing Grace, how sweet thy name. Amaz- -zing Grace. Wisps of cloud clinging to his head, Hieronymous burst out of a slit in the sky, zooming down to where the boy with the girl clinging to his back were plowing through the brine.

"So there you are, my dears," said the bird, as if not a day had passed since they last had parted. "I've come for you, children. Had an exciting journey, have you?"

The girl laughed. The boy, not knowing exactly what to do, smiled. The boy and the girl pulled themselves onto Hieronymous's sturdy wings. The girl felt the familiar rush of wind in her face, and though she knew she was again human, she was also something more that had no name. The boy felt as though a huge powerful bird was beating its wings inside his chest, and the girl agreed. At that moment, they both gazed down at their lost and found hearts.

VIII
Tale Without End

In the way that a snake can swallow its own tail, the girl arrived back at the shores of the old kingdom. The Queen, her mother, had died. Princess N had married one, two, three gentlemen, and since none of them had proven themselves worthy, according to her standards, she decided to live alone, surrounded by the wealth of her one, two, and three husbands.

Rumors spread that she was as miserable was ever and blamed anyone in her sight for her miseries.

In short, the entire kingdom was in shambles. The girl had no desire to move back into the palace, which was now the home of spiders and roaches and bats. It seemed as if decades and decades had passed. The palace grounds badly needed tending. Thick-necked weeds and briars choked the gardens. The groomed lawns grew into waist-high meadows spiked with warrior thistles, mustard weed, and wild rose. Even so, as the girl stamped her way through the undergrowth, a small pleasure began to take shape in the pit of her being. The pleasure grew, prompting her to run down to the river, swinging her arms and singing.

Nothing about the river had changed. It was as she remembered it: a brushstroke of ebony bubbling and rippling over smooth white stones. The air smelled of damp moss and the vegetal mineral odor of the water. She looked up. The sky was egg-shell blue with streaks of tangerine where the sun perched. The girl sat down on the bank and dipped her toes into the icy stream. In her front pocket she carried a tiny red silk purse given to her by the boy, which now she opened on her lap. She took from it a tuft of his golden hair, sniffing and stroking the fine strands. Dreamily, she remembered his words.

"You have restored my life to me and in return I give you this—a piece of myself for you to carry next to your heart. If ever you are lost, or torn apart as I have been, call to me and I will come to you and help. Know this is a pledge for life."

From her other pocket, the girl extracted a bird's feather.

"Dear girl," Hieronymous had said, "remember there will always be a bird alive inside you. Remember the clouds and the stars are your home as well as the earth. Remember you can fly." Because her heart was full, with love and sorrow, she sang: *Amaz-zing Grace, how sweet thy name.*

A breeze lifted off the river carrying her song with it so that her words tinkled in the leafy trees, a choir of tiny bells. A dusty-looking horse with a low-slung haunch stood down river. He appeared like an apparition, growing more solid as the mist above the eddies drifted away. The girl slid off the bank. Carrying her shoes and the red purse, she hop-scotched from rock to rock until she reached the horse. He waited for her, silently. Burying her face in his flank, she felt a joy like homecoming.

The horse nuzzled her hair and whinnied. Very tenderly, he asked, "And do you know the trap? And do you know its true name?" It was the mink's voice. The girl raised her head from the horse's neck. The horse beamed.

"Name the trap by its true name," she shouted, "and you will be free."

Then, in a slightly formal manner, she recited to the horse what she had learned.

"The name of the trap is my name. My old name, that is, Littlest Princess and also Princess Please-Her. For that is who I thought I was, and in thinking so, became so, and so was trapped. Now I know who I am." Here she giggled and nuzzled the horse who whinnied his agreement. "I am Mink and Bird-Girl and Friend-of-Boy, Heart-Retriever, and so many more."

"Yes, even more," said the horse, "as I am mink and heron, cheetah and she-bear, and more."

The horse invited the girl to climb onto his back. She laced her fingers through his mane and hung on as he galloped out past the borders of the palace, out into the highlands carpeted with heather and gorse. The horse gained speed, and the girl laid her head on his neck, her hair and the horse's mane whipping the wind. The honeybees broadcast

Princess with Horses

their concertos, and the deer stood at the edge of the forest, a low humming in their throats. The girl cried out, "I have found my true home. I know who I am. My name is Princess Every-Name."

The End

The Littlest Princess Who Found Her Name – A Tale of Individuation

By Murray Stein

Introduction

This fairy tale is about a Princess who must find her true name. One has a name given by mother and father at birth, and one has an immortal name given by the Self before birth. The first belongs to the body and to temporality; the second belongs to the soul and eternity. As we have two personalities within us—the one conscious, the other unconscious—so we have two handles. "We are that pair of Dioscuri, one of whom is mortal and the other immortal,"[1] as Jung declares to the astonishment of his audience at the Eranos Conference in 1939: we are Castor *and* Pollux, the twin sons of Leda with two fathers, King Tyndareus and Zeus. The first is a social and temporal aspect of the personality—persona, ego-consciousness, whose identity is formed by family and cultural matrix. The second is archetypal and eternal, whose identity emerges during life from the collective unconscious. The first is given at birth and learned by the child; the second is discovered within, often in the second half of life. This fairy tale is the story of a shift from the first identity to the second, from being located purely in a social matrix to being grounded in the archetypal Self.

I will treat this work by Dale Kushner as a classic fairy tale and not as a personal story about Dale's life as an American woman of a certain time, as an accomplished poet and novelist, a wife and a mother. Instead, I will discuss it an archetypal story of individuation, therefore applicable to many individuals in far-flung latitudes and cultures. Fairy tales tell of general types and themes that belong to the common heritage of humanity and represent psychological issues that apply to everyone, not only to a unique individual. The characters in fairy tales typically carry no personal or family names, only general designations like "princess," "prince," "woodcutter," etc. As the great interpreter of fairy tales, Marie-Louise von Franz writes, fairy tales "are the purest and simplest expression of collective unconscious psychic processes."[2] They are not about idiosyncratic neuroses rooted in unique life experiences of the individual, nor are they limited to specific cultural complexes or patterns. They are spun of motifs that are archetypal and arise from the collective unconscious, which means they are universal and apply to people in all times and places. "In myths and fairy tales, as in dreams, the psyche tells its own story, and the interplay of the archetypes is revealed in its natural setting as 'formation, transformation / the eternal Mind's eternal recreation,"[3] writes Jung in his essay on "The Phenomenology of the Spirit Fairytales." For reflecting on fairytales, I have found M.-L. von Franz's *Introduction to the Interpretation of Fairytales* most useful as a guide ever since I first attended her lectures on which this book is based fifty years ago at the Jung Institute in Zurich.

"The Littlest Princess" is, unlike the fairy tales collected by the Brothers Grimm and others, a story written by an individual with a unique personality and history at a specific time and place, but the fairy tale Dale has written down on paper is not about only her life experiences and personal issues, which to some degree is the case too of course. It is rather much more: it is about Everywoman. It has all the characteristic features of the fairy tale—anonymous characters, archetypal motifs and developments, and a successful lysis. As a story of transformation from one stage of life to another, it is "ever-living like all fairytales, and ... contains the quintessence and deepest meaning of the Hermetic mystery"[4] of transformation, which human beings in all times and places have used as resources for guidance and wisdom since time immemorial.

This fairy tale, moreover, shows the classic three-part pattern of initiations as described by anthropologists Arnold van Gennep and Victor Turner: separation, liminality, re-entry. As I have written in my book, *In MidLife*, I understand these phases to provide a passage from stages of life embedded in the "Mother World" and the "Father World" (family of origin, culture) to an individual sense of identity given through the mystery of transformation that takes place during the transition from first to second half of life. This leads to re-entry into social life and the collective as a "new person" with a sense of identity rooted deeply in the Self rather than in the social persona. It is a movement from dependence on rules and repression of unacceptable aspects of psyche to personal freedom and individual responsibility, and it has the effect of transforming fate into chosen destiny.

Stage One – Separation

The fairy tale begins with establishing the setting and dramatis personae.

> *Once there lived a queen and her daughter, Princess N. The Queen loved her daughter, but she also envied her. She envied the princess her eyes, which had not yet seen sorrow; she envied the princess her laugh, which bubbled forth at the slightest merriment. She even envied the princess her sleep, which was the sleep of animals safe in their lair. But what the Queen envied most was the princess's life, which was just beginning to unfold.*

"The Littlest Princess" opens with a Queen mother and her female child in a hostile embrace. The Queen is conflicted in her attitude toward her daughter, her maternal feelings contradicted by her narcissistic personality. There is no King in the story. The masculine principle is missing, and the Youngest Princess is born to the Queen as though parthenogenically, without reference to a father.

The mother's motive is totally egocentric: she wants to forestall awareness of her finitude.

The emotional tone in this asymmetrical matriarchal family is darkly colored by envy. The presence of the evil eye of envy is all pervasive, cast on the heroine not only by the older sister but then also by the Queen mother. The life of the Littlest Princess turns into imprisonment in a golden cage where she is tortured continuously by the envy attacks of sister and mother. It is well known to psychotherapists that often "the nastiest envy attacks take place within the supposedly cozy sanctuaries of immediate and extended family networks."[5] The Littlest Princess finds no refuge in this contaminated world, and so she turns to imagination, to the archetypal image of the Goddess, the Moon-Maiden, for comfort.

> *On those nights when the Littlest Princess could not sleep—for sleep meant falling into a pit crowded with demons—she rose from her bed to gaze out the window where the moon balanced delicately above the highest mountain. "Moon-Maiden, Moon-Maiden" she sang, "how far away you are. Moon-Maiden, Moon-Maiden,*

come for me now." Long into the night, the Littlest Princess would sing her song until the birds stirring among the silver leaves, added their voices to hers. The Moon-Maiden, however, never answered and gave no sign she heard the Littlest Princess.

Although unsuccessful at first, this turn-away from immediate social reality to imagination will prove decisive for the liberation and development of the heroine.

The stage has been set the for the break-away that follows. When mother becomes negative, child must separate and find a way to freedom. Conversely, if mother does not turn negative, child runs the risk of remaining fused with her, dependent on her largess, an eternal child (puella aeterna or puer aeternus). In this fairy tale, the Queen attempts to keep her daughters dependent, again for purely egocentric reasons. She becomes the "devouring mother" or "witch," that Hans Dieckmann writes about: "The witch is an evil, demonic mother figure who uses the children's hunger to entice them into her power to hold them captive, to exploit their labor...for highly egoist ends, and ultimately to devour them."[6] The Littlest Princess begs for deliverance, both external and internal, from devouring mother and envious sister, and the unconscious responds by sending a helpful animal.

It was noted earlier that there is no father in the environment of the negative mother/sister pair. It is an asymmetrical matriarchal set-up featuring a Queen and no King. If there is a father about somewhere, he is insignificant and of no use to his troubled daughter. M.L. von Franz suggests looking at the beginning and the end of fairy tales to see what is missing at the outset and added at the conclusion. As we will see in this story, symmetry is established at the level of the Princess (but not for the Queen mother or the sister) toward the end. This fairy tale world does not transform from matriarchal to patriarchal, which is the usual pattern of development according to Erich Neumann.[7] Instead, it leaps over the patriarchal to the individual stage of development, which we might think of a function of *sublimatio*, a leap over an intermediate stage to a final one. This leap has important cultural relevance today when political movements in the West show strong tendencies toward the restoration of traditional patriarchal social structure.

The archetypal role of the father in the individuation process is to assist the child, whether girl or boy, in separating from the nurturing "mother-world" of the original family and entering the more demanding world of adulthood—"love and work"—with a sense of responsibility and self-sustainability. For a daughter, this transformation typically occurs via the Oedipal (or rather Electra) triangle; for the son, it occurs when son idealizes father as a role model. If the father figure is absent, the young person will have to rely on the unconscious to provide a way forward. This may happen through projection of the archetypal father image onto another person in the environment or via imagination. In this story, the Littlest Princess turns directly to the archetypal world available to imagination,

Stage Two – Liminality and Initiations

The First Initiation

> *One evening when the pear trees in the garden showed their frilly blossoms and the pussy willows wore their early fur, as the Littlest Princess perched on her window seat ready to sing to the Moon-Maiden, she noticed a shadow*

sliding over the white pebbles on the path below. The shadow moved like a breeze over water, vanishing before the princess could even open her mouth. "Perhaps it is only the night-faces of the roses nodding to each other under the moonlight," she thought. "Or the willow saplings, dipping to kiss the edge of the river." The Littlest Princess leaned further out her window. The moon shone like the inside of an oyster shell. "I must be imagining it," she sighed. "There is no one among the irises and roses. The night is as lonely as I." But just as she said those very words, two yellow eyes winked up at her from the darkness, and before she could string together another sentence, the shadow was strutting across her windowsill in the form of a mink.

An imaginal conversation opens the relation to the animal, and the human form of the Princess suddenly transforms into a mirror image of the animal. She identifies with the previously unconscious instinct. This is the first initiation.

The Princess's energy now shifts away from perceptions of the surrounding social world of mother and sister to the strong instinctual energy that will take her on a journey into the unknown animal world. This encounter with the shadow is a typical beginning of active imagination. Psychological identification with unconscious figures brings excitement and energy but also danger. Shadow here is presented as a positive source of energy opening an avenue of escape from persona entrapment. The mink represents instinctual erotic energy that has been denied the Princess in the matriarchal world dominated by mother and sister, and she is now about to integrate it into her conscious life. Separating from the conventional life she has known, she is on her own as she scampers away into the forest.

The transformation into an animal means that the Princess is now reliant on her instincts, not on cues from others around her. She has discovered and strongly identified with feminine sexuality. This initiation of women was celebrated in ancient Roman times at the Villa of Mysteries outside of Pompeii and took place under the aegis of Dionysos, the god of wine, ecstasy and sensuality. In his commentary on the visions of Christiana Morgan,

Jung says: "It was very important in the initiation that the initiate should remember where [s]he was still identical with the animal, to walk on the animal path, as it were, in order to reach nature again from within...they felt once more the influx of the god, a renewed power, the immortal power of nature."[8] This is what the Princess is experiencing as she separates from her previous life as a conventional daughter and sister.

The helpful animal is a classic feature of fairy tales and represents the willingness of the somatic unconscious to introduce a person to the challenging process of individuation. When the Princess responds positively to the offer of the animal, she is accepting initiation into womanhood. Her previous identity dissolves, and she is released from the prison of convention. She can go on a journey of her own, independent of her restrictive mother and envious sister, and at first this seems delightful and filled with joy but then turns threatening as all initiation rituals do. As Joseph Henderson has written, initiations must include the "ordeal." This feature is written into the script of initiation ceremonies and rituals.[9] Frequently this involves near death experiences, and at the minimum it includes frightening challenges to the initiate. We can see the "ordeal" vividly depicted in the pictures on the walls of the Villa of Mysteries and discussed by Linda Fierz-David in her book, *The Women's Dionysian Initiation: The Villa of Mysteries in Pompeii*.

Understandably, beautiful Princess-Mink becomes the target of hunters. What a trophy she would be, they think quietly to themselves when they spot her in her fine coat of glossy fur. Suddenly, it appears the Princess has fallen out of the restrictive mother-pan into the fires of a dangerous world. She could be shot and skinned for the pleasure of these hunters, presumably males. To escape them, she disappears into a nearby river, which at first seems delicious and secure but then empties into the sea where the immensity and power of the huge waves overwhelm her. The easy, defensive escape maneuver is not a solution to her dilemma, and as she climbs back to land severe loneliness sets in. She has reached the limits of her ability to explore the world as a mink. The loneliness that ensues is typical of a phase in the experience of liminality. One is betwixt-and-between, alone, and has not yet found a sustaining symbol that will answer the fundamental question, "What is my name?"

The experience of loneliness is a common experience in the individuation process as it enters territories that are not commonly understood by other members of collective society. Many people who engage in deep inner work report that they soon find themselves without companions. Suspicions about their own sanity begin to infect them. They become increasingly isolated in their experience of life because they carry a secret within themselves. Their search for symbol and meaning is foreign to the collectives they live in. The only suitable companion on this journey lives in the inner world.

Bird-Girl – the Second Transformation

Suddenly, as she is despairing, Princess-Mink spots a strange-looking object that looks like an umbrella stuck in the sand but turns out to be an ibis-like bird. As Jung observes, in fairy tales "in the supreme moment something helpful appears."[10] If the mink grounded the Princess in body and instinct, the bird, a heron, will elevate her to spirit. Again, the Princess accepts the invitation to continue her brave venture into the unknown. At the heron's invitation, she climbs on his back, and he takes her into up into the clouds.

> *"Howdy-do. Name's Hieronymous," the voice said as they swept through the belly of a cloud. Hieronymous, the Princess-Mink decided, was a sleek machine. Awkward on land, he flew effortlessly through the air. In a few minutes, her body relaxed. She had to admit, she was enjoying herself. The sea shone below and the sky above.*

This is a second intervention of the unconscious to assist the heroine's journey to individuation.

The name of this figure comes as a surprise to the reader of fairy tales. Characters are not typically given a name in fairy tales. They are identified simply by role. A masculine figure, Hieronymous introduces a tone of lightness, affability, and musical playfulness. He comes singing in accents that sound of the South. There is something African about him, perhaps akin to the ancient Egyptian ibis god, Thoth, the lord of scribes and writers. And art attaches to the name. It brings immediate associations to the Dutch painter, Hieronymus Bosch. The name is also a form of Jerome, the masterful translator of the Holy Scriptures into Latin. Altogether, Hieronymous, the heron, represents a spiritual function (the animus) that elevates consciousness to the divine and symbolizes a connection to immortality and eternity. This figure is prepared not only to rescue Princess-Mink but to take her up out of the earthy animal-instinct realm into the highest regions of spirit.

The Princess's second transformation follows quickly. Hieronymous teaches her to use her arms as wings, and as she does so she becomes a bird with white feathers, a strong symbol of the spiritualization process. In alchemy, this is the product of the operation, *sublimatio*, the transformation of solid material to gas without passing through the liquid state. In this operation, the soul is extracted from the material base to which it had become attached (*unio naturalis*) and united with spirit to create the *unio mentalis*. With *unio mentalis* as platform, one can see far, beyond the immediate issues of the moment and the day. "With wings we can look at things from both the perspective of earth and heaven at the same time. Intuition and inspiration seem to arrive unexpectedly on wings out of thin air..."[11] The soul becomes wedded to the spirit. This results in exaltation, a sense of higher meaning, the conscious participation in one's personal destiny. It is a stage in the development toward full psychological wholeness.

The heroine in her feathered coat and flying high beside Hieronymous as her companion now can see far. As she wings above the sea, she notices a round object bobbing in the waters below, which turns out to be a severed head calling for help. Her compassionate response to this cry for help will become the most critical action in her individuation journey.

Sheer spirituality offers no final solution to the deepest problems raised by the process of psychological individuation because it overrides the unconscious call for attention to the psychic body that was left behind to achieve *unio mentalis.* The state of mind achieved in spirituality must now attend to the left-behind psychic body, its shadow. This is the next stage of individuation according to Jung as discussed in the final chapter of his last major book, *Mysterium Coniunctionis.* Mind and body must be re-united after their separation to achieve the state of complete unity that is the goal of the alchemical process.

And this task is precisely what Bird-Girl is now called upon to undertake. She must descend from the heights and dive deeply into the waters of the unconscious to complete her work before she can return to her Kingdom.

> *"Hieronymous," she yelled. "Hieronymous, there is something in the sea that is calling to us."*

Hieronymous the heron is not interested. The sea is full of flotsam and jetsam. Why bother? Hieronymous speaks for the purely spiritual:

> *"Nonsense," said he. "It is only the sun reflecting on a bed of weeds. I've seen it a hundred times. The sun and the sea play tricks together. It's nothing, I tell you. Nothing at all."*

But Bird-Girl is not convinced. Here she separates her judgment from the voice of the authoritative spiritual guide. She listens with her heart.

> *Not satisfied, her heart leading her in another direction, the Bird-Girl circled back toward the mysterious object, which she saw now was not a golden orb at all, but the head of a boy whose pale hair caught and held the sunlight. The boy's face was the picture of consternation. She flew closer. He*

> *was trying to talk, but each time he opened his mouth, sea water poured in, and he sputtered. The Bird-Girl's heart filled with pity. She remembered the awkwardness of her minkself in the sea. She circled still lower until she was almost directly above the head and was able to hear his words:*
>
> *"Been torn apart. Arms, legs, torso, all lost at sea. Help me. Help me please. Find all my pieces. Bring them back to me so I can be whole again."*

Who is this dismembered boy whose head is floating on the waves? He is the dismembered pieces of the Princess's masculine counterpart, the other side of her personality. In this dismembered youth, she finds the element that was missing in the Queen's realm—the masculine. This has been dismembered by an unknown power (the Queen Mother's animus?) and thrown into the sea, in other words deeply repressed by the forces of family and culture. At the beginning, there was no father and no brother. And princesses cannot think for themselves! They must ask others what to think, what to say, and how to act in their prescribed role. This is the trap the Littlest Princess escaped from, and now, with a great deal of toil and endurance, she can put the pieces of her dismembered animus together again. She is restoring what was once a unity, a syzygy, then was broken asunder and the masculine part shattered and repressed by collective voices. This created the trap of rigid one-sidedness that we saw at the outset. Now the heroine can gather the pieces and restore the boy's body (and her psyche) to its fullness. She will establish symmetry through this extremely demanding *opus.*

> *Seeing how the head struggled to keep afloat, the Bird-Girl understood the importance of the boy's body. "Surely a head needs a body, for what good is a head without all the other parts?"*

She manages to gather the trunk and the limbs, and the hardest to locate is the missing heart, which has been captured by a mysterious ghost who lives in a cave at the very bottom of the sea. This demon longs for a heart but is himself locked in a suit of armor that makes it impossible for him to integrate one. He has a large collection on the shelf, but they are no use. He is beyond hope and has become cold and isolated. He is a collector of hearts, a familiar type of psychopathic character, seeking love but unable to experience it. I surmise this is the Queen Mother's lethal cold animus. The Princess, steeling herself against the temptation to find compassion for this lost soul, retrieves the boy's heart from the demon's storeroom and brings it to the now reassembled body of the youth. This is her triumph. Because she felt compassion for the boy's suffering with her heart, she was able to discover and retrieve his heart from the depths of the sea. It is akin to what the Taoists call "the heart of the heart." It reaches far beyond sentimentality and romantic love. It links her, through him, to the Self.

Stage Three – Re-entry

Mission accomplished, it is time to return to the Kingdom the Princess left a time ago. She is no longer mink or bird. She has taken back her human form as a woman, but she is inwardly transformed. The scene with the restored youth is movingly tender as he offers to accompany her on her journey home:

> *When he was wholly composed once again, arms, the boy addressed the girl with compassion. "And where will you go now?" he asked.*
>
> *The girl was touched by his kindness. She had become accustomed to his*

> *brusque manner and desperate commands. "I will try to make my way across the sea," she said, "but since I no longer have wings to fly, or special lungs or gills and fins with which to swim it will be a very slow journey to the other side of the sea."*
>
> *The boy and the girl lay on their backs, floating. The boy nodded, his golden hair spilling out in a halo of light. The two were very quiet.*
>
> *"Let us stay together a little longer," said the boy. "Whilst one of us swims, the other can sleep on the swimmer's back. When we reach the nearest shore, we can part ways and say good-bye."*
>
> *The girl was agreeable and so they began their journey following the sun across the sky.*

The girl has achieved the re-union with the lost part of the psyche, and this constitutes her individuation journey's climax. She is now Ready and fully prepared to claim her place in the collective as a free and creative personality. She has found her name in the multitude of identities she has experienced in her journey: Princess Every-Name.

This return to everyday life is beautifully depicted in the famous Zen Buddhist Ox-Herding Pictures. After the recovery of his lost ox, the ox-herder experiences enlightenment, the highest state of consciousness in the Zen tradition. But this is not the end of the story. The final image in the series shows him as sage returning to the marketplace, where trees and flowers bloom wherever he goes and where he becomes a teacher to the young. This will be the future destiny of our heroine (and the fairy tale's author as well), perhaps in a next installment.

After the journey through liminality, the heroine returns to her home, which has in the meantime also changed significantly. Her mother is dead, her sister is living miserably in depression and isolation, and the Princess is free to choose her destiny as she will. Her re-entry is grounded in a sense of identity that knows the complex reality of the psyche. She remembers her life as mink and as bird. And she finds a source of useful energy in the form of another friendly animal, a horse:

> *The horse invited the girl to climb onto*
> *his back. She laced her fingers through*

> *his mane and hung on as he galloped out past the borders of the palace, out into the highlands carpeted with heather and gorse. The horse gained speed, and the girl laid her head on his neck, her hair and the horse's mane whipping the wind. The honeybees broadcast their concertos, and the deer stood at the edge of the forest, a low humming in their throats. The girl cried out, "I have found my true home. I know who I am. My name is Princess Every-Name."*

The flexibility offered by this realization will keep her free of entrapment in a singular collective persona. She can be herself in whatever context she chooses. In psychological terms, she has united conscious and unconscious personalities to such a degree that she is protected from collective entrapments. Princess Every-Name will be her secret ineffable name and hers alone.

Conclusion

What can people gain from reading fairy tales like this? Fairy tales are like dreams, messages from the unconscious that offer the one-sidedness of ego-consciousness a compensatory vision of the psyche's reality and potential. Traditionally, they have been shared in communities. People repeat stories handed down through the generations that offer psychological guidance and wisdom. Individuals and collectives inevitably get stuck in ironclad habits of mind and heart. They stagnate, become discouraged and hopeless, sometimes even suicidal. The compensatory messages from the unconscious open the mind's windows and doors and reveal potentials for growth, for further exploration and development. People are offered a map for individuation that aims for the mysterious goal of wholeness. They are released from their cages and can move forward creatively.

We see this clearly in "The Littlest Princess." The story shows a way to individuation from a state of "stuck with a restrictive persona" to freedom and creativity. It is an age-old story found in all cultures because it is fundamentally human. The story offers the reader wise guidance. It's a map for the soul's journey through life.

Endnotes

[1] C.G. Jung, "Concerning Rebirth," para. 235.

[2] M.-L. von Franz, "Introduction to the Interpretation of Fairytales," p. 1.

[3] C.G. Jung, "The Phenomenology of the Spirit in Fairytales," para. 400.

[4] C.G. Jung, "The Spirit Mercurius," para. 239.

[5] M. Stein, "The Problem of Envy and Sibling Rivalry," p. 115.

[6] H. Dieckmann, *Twice-Told Tales*, pp. 34-35.

[7] See E. Neumann, *The Origins and History of Consciousness.*

[8] C.G. Jung, *Visions*, vol. 1, p. 151.

[9] J. Henderson, *Thresholds of Initiation*, pp. 89ff.

[10] Ibid., p. 166.

[11] ARAS, *The Book of Symbols*, p. 240.

References

Archive for Research on Archetypal Symbolism. (2010). *The Book of Symbols. Reflections on Archetypal Images*. Edited by A. Ronnberg and K. Martin. Taschen America.

Dieckmann, H. (1978/1986). *Twice-Told Tales. The Psychological Use of Fairy Tales*. Asheville, NC: Chiron Publications.

Fierz-David, L. and N. Hall. (2005). *Dreaming in Red: The Women's Dionysian Initiation Chamber in Pompeii*. Putnam, CT: Spring Publications.

Henderson, J. (1967/2005). *Thresholds of Initiation*. Asheville, NC: Chiron Publications.

Jung, C.G. (1948/1967). "The Spirit Mercurius." In *Collected Works*, vol. 13. Princeton, NJ: Princeton University Press.

____. (1948/1969). "The Phenomenology of the Spirit in Fairytales." In *Collected Works*, vol. 9i. Princeton, NJ: Princeton University Press.

____. (1950/1969). "Concerning Rebirth." In

Collected Works, vol. 9i. Princeton, NJ: Princeton University Press.

____. (1955/1963). *Mysterium Coniunctionis.* In *Collected Works,* vol. 14. Princeton, NJ: Princeton University Press.

____. (1997). *Visions: Notes of the Seminar Given in 1930-1934.* Edited by Claire Douglas. Princeton, NJ: Princeton University Press.

Neumann, E. (1949/1973). *The Origins and History of Consciousness.* Princeton, NJ: Princeton University Press.

Stein, M. (1983/2003/2014). *In MidLife. A Jungian Perspective.* Asheville, NC: Chiron Publications.

____. (1990/2022). "The Problem of Envy and Sibling Rivalry." In *Collected Writings,* vol. 4. Asheville, NC: Chiron Publications.

Von Franz, M.-L. (2023). "Introduction to the Interpretation of Fairytales." In *Collected Works,* vol. 8. Asheville, NC: Chiron Publications.

The Song of Every-Name: Reflections on The Littlest Princess

By Dariane Pictet

Once upon a time, there is a Queen and the King is nowhere to be seen. His absence presses upon the world. In that hollow space, the Mother swells—untethered. The Queen's love curdles into a hunger for her daughter's aliveness.

Then she longs for another child—not for its own sake, but to escape death. Her love is crooked, ambivalent, a sweetened poison. Princess N, the elder, suffers her mother's coldness, watching her coo over the newborn. A field of envy grows in the Queen, its roots coiling into the soul of the elder daughter, who turns her sharpness on her sister. Through stories of ogres and monsters, unconscious fears and disowned aggression become palpable presences in the palace. Two sisters orbit the

Queen's need like trapped moons and vanish into her shadow, losing the memory of their true name.

For the Littlest Princess, the psyche's most vulnerable part—the child who still loves and longs without defense—the experience is bewildering. The fault must surely lie within herself. And she learns the ancient art of pleasing: a magic that hides the self so well even the heart forgets its true shape.

There is a pattern—especially in the feminine experience—of subsisting through compliance to an ideal, attempting to win back love through submission, compliance and invisibility. It is the trance of virtue, the dream of being "chosen" at the cost of one's own life force. Marion Woodman calls this the *addiction to perfection*—the internalized belief: *If I am good enough, quiet enough, beautiful enough... Then I will be cherished.* It is the child's logic in the face of narcissistic wounding: *If Mother cannot love me, the fault must be mine.*

The Littlest Princess turns her longing toward the Moon Maiden; the silent, celestial presence who watches over the night. The Moon Maiden offers beauty and mystery to a lonely child, but no reply. A reflection of Mother, without arms to hold her, yet unwaveringly there.

The Queen, gripped by the fear of death, grows increasingly controlling. She tries to forestall mortality by keeping the girls—embodiments of youth and life—perpetually within her sight. Without them, she would lose her own fragile sense of vitality. Thus she becomes ever more suffocating: love transforms into possession; care into captivity.

In her loneliness and despair, the Littlest Princess—burdened by the impossibility of pleasing—utters a wish from the depths of her soul, a quiet, inner whisper: to become invisible. A yearning to step out of the pressure to conform, and to live for others' approval; a self that she has worn like a suit of armor, hiding the torment of not being reflected for who she is.

This wish does not go unheard. Lurking at the edge of the forest is Mink—keeper of the instinctual and wild—a liminal creature, secretive and elusive, inhabiting the thresholds between worlds. The mink carries the wisdom of concealment—he embodies the knowledge that authenticity sometimes requires withdrawal from the collective gaze.

"They see you for what you are not," the mink says solemnly, "and not for what you are. To please is to lie—a trap you lie in." With these words, the spell of adaptation begins to break. The desire to please—once a survival strategy—is unmasked as a prison of the soul. The trap that binds the soul long after Mother has vanished from view, and contracts into a persona, built to survive conditional love. And the deeper snare lies in the belief that love must be earned by self-erasure. *And do you know its true name?* Its true name is self-betrayal. The chains that bound her were woven from the false perceptions she carried like a twisted secret.

To preserve her own becoming, she must risk departure. She recognizes—in the instinctual wisdom of the soul—that life demands separation. The longing that once sought safety and belonging now becomes the impetus for flight. In choosing invisibility, the Littlest Princess slips beneath the surface of social identity.

She changes her name to Princess-Mink—furred, low to the earth, clever and agile. She enters the world of nature—the wild terrain beyond the walls of the mother's palace. Here, in the solitude of forests and rivers, she learns to move unseen, to dwell in silence, to shed the compulsion to mirror others' desires.

It is a period of renewal, of reconnection with the animal soul—a return to the primal, unfiltered part of herself, that layer of being closest to the ground, to body, to survival wisdom, and the quiet knowledge of self-preservation. In her running, she understands that the wound had never been hers to blame on another. It was passed down—through glance and gesture, doors closed a little too hard, smiles that didn't reach the eyes. Love flickered, conditional as weather. Envy drifted like a chill, rage gathered in corners whilst the palace held its breath. And she, small and watchful, learned to feel the storm before it broke. She mistook inheritance for identity—believing the sadness in the room was hers, the sharp looks deserved, the silence a sign she had failed. The emotions passed down became the threads she wove into a self. What was ancestral, she called personal. What was transmitted, she called true.

Princess-Mink moves through shadowed places—between darkness and light, between the grounded earth and the boundless heaven, and hears the call of flight, the ascent into the free sky of spirit. The bird Hieronymous speaks of winds that carry far beyond the reach of the earth. His holy name evokes the sacred law of her being. His voice, sweet and full of promise, sings of wider horizons and invites her to shed her fur and take to the air.

With him, she grows feathers and becomes Bird-Girl—and tastes the wind-born joy of flying, soaring high above the clouds. Hieronymous reminds her that the journey toward self-discovery is a sacred task, and that to find freedom, she must first obey the laws of her own being. In her flight, she finds perspective and humour. *"Oh surely this must be freedom," thought the Princess-Mink, whose joy at that moment was as boundless as the sky. "I did not know there is a bird alive inside me."* He helps her navigate through the fog of self-doubt that clouds her sense of identity to find something alive and fresh within.

Hieronymous leaves her with a warning that she has learned to fly but the sky is not her home, and that she must not falter in a mission that she must accomplish alone.

Bird-Girl, who sees from above, with sky-thought and feathered sight, journeys on. In the foaming sea, she finds him—a Boy torn apart, limbs scattered like forgotten dreams. His eyes gleam with the coldness of fractured intent. His voice, raw and jagged, cuts through the stillness with the sharpness of command. He demands help.

His head, distant and half-sunk in the ocean, holds a look of defiance—a gaze that says, gather my missing pieces—heart, arms, legs—you must find me, for I am incomplete without you. He mirrors the wounds she cannot avoid, not now, not—the unwept, unburied, unnamed. The brokenness before her is not his alone; it echoes an ancestral grief felt in her bones—a summons from the past, to be counted and included in the unfolding consciousness.

He compels her with an urgency impossible to ignore and pushes her into the fire of her own uncertainty. His presence is a reminder that the path to wholeness is not one of comfort, but of confrontation.

Boy's hardness is his only shield. This is how the exiled masculine survives: by testing love before it will trust. He is not to be healed by softness, but by the ruthless gathering of pieces, one by one. For it is said that for a man to be a man, he must feel the bitter taste of failure, he must kill the hero in himself. His brokenness, scattered across the sea land, reminds us of the violence that the wounded masculine has reaped upon the world—a shadow that demands reckoning.

The masculine does not die, it shatters. It becomes what it has learned: Cold. Demanding. The animus in a woman's psyche appears as a harsh critic, a tyrant, an inner bully. It becomes hostile, arrogant or violent when it is not balanced by the softening integration of the feminine values. It may also take refuge in an impotent attitude, filled with judgment and despair, a withdrawn ghost, silent and aloof.

The Boy's fragmentation reflects both personal trauma—twisted and scarred—and the cultural wounding of the masculine, shaped by aggressive one-sidedness. His crudeness shatters her illusions, forcing her beyond the projections born of an absent, idealized father. This is a confrontation with pain and an opportunity for an embodied act of reparation.

This is the state of many women (and men!) before their inner work: they flee into instinct and material comfort (Mink). They flee into disembodied flight (Bird), in the pursuit of ungrounded spiritual pursuits. But these are temporary shelters. Release—but not yet a deliverance, not the deeper connection Bird-Girl truly needs. Without a sense of purpose, this freedom risks being fleeting, a momentary high rather than a lasting change. It may become a trap that could slip into chaos or addiction, or an ecstatic but hollow spiritual pursuit. She could soar, untethered from the very self she seeks to reclaim—an escape from her old life, yes, but still an avoidance from the reality of her wounds.

And in the tale, these wounds become scattered parts—a dismembered figure, a soul in fragments, the lost limbs of the masculine self. The Littlest Princess's transformations—Princess-Mink and Bird-Girl—are ne-cessary preparations for the healing of the dismembered Boy. His command is a call to purpose. This journey takes her back through all the places where love faltered—where the word cut instead of comforted, where the hand struck or withdrew, where the father was absent or annihilating, where the sister brother mocked or fell silent.

It is no small task. It is a long work. Slow. Uneven. Marked by failure as much as progress. This is not merely an act of rescue, but a healing within herself and in the world.

Each piece must be searched for—collecting the lost parts of the screaming Boy, lost at sea, means integrating vision, action, inspiration, dialogue, and—crucially—direction. For it is true that the Boy needs a goal to develop and it may take a long time before it reveals itself.

As the Littlest Princess gathered the pieces, beneath the water, in dark forests, in forgotten corners of memory, she feels not just the weight of each fragment, but the burden of her alienation. Each limb she returns to him is a step closer to herself, a stitch in the wound she had long ignored. And so she endures—the stops and starts, the failures, the doubts—because something in her knows that this is what heals the split between being and doing, between the soul's fluid depths and the world's sharp edges.

She recovers his lost vision—and a clarity of purpose. And with his restored gaze, he sees not just the world—but himself within it. A felt sense of being here, real, and responsive.

With his arms, she restores agency—the ability to reach, to shape, to touch life with intention. With his legs, denied movement and unclaimed action return and the ability to move toward life, not away from it.

What was once fragmented is made whole—not in perfection, but in participation. He belongs again—to the world, to the moment, to himself.

Finally, in a jar, hidden deep, she finds his heart — sealed in glass, untouched, still beating with the pulse of what was lost.

She places the heart, once silent, now whispered of pain and longing, back into the now remembered boy. His form, once jagged and shattered, begins to shift. His eyes, that burned with the bitterness of loss, sparkle with the understanding of what it means to be both broken and mended. His voice, gentle like the first whispers of dawn, speaks in the soft tones of one who has been healed by facing the hurt. The dissonance that had lived in him—the anger—dissolves so that he may serve life, not defend against it.

And when the work is done, the dominating tyrant who demeaned her becomes the man she had longed for—who could walk with her. Man. Protector. Builder. Guide. Lover of life. The restored, integrated animus becomes kind, he inspires and offers devotion. He the inner guide, the bridge to Spirit. And in finding him, she has come home to herself.

His parting gift was a piece of himself to carry next to her heart. As he pressed his promise into her chest, unsaid but felt—a warm pulse against her own—that sounded something like; you need never wander lost again. I am here—your voice, your sword, your true North.

It is a promise that she cradles within her, the strength, clarity, and loyalty of the healed masculine. This is the symbol of an enduring partnership.

Jung might say this is the moment when the ego—purified by ordeal, humbled by love, and strengthened through encounter with the Other—is no longer inflated nor diminished. It has found its place in relation to the Self, that center, which holds all opposites.

She has integrated the wounded masculine not by submission to his raw power, nor by rejecting him as an enemy, but by the work of love: the gathering, the healing, the patient mending of what was broken.

In doing so, she had claimed the hidden partner who lives within every woman—who grants not domination, but direction; not conquest, but dialogue. This is the positive animus—the critical voice or the seducer of impossible ideals transformed into a loyal inner companion, who protects and strengthens one's becoming. The Princess and the Boy are the two halves of a single being: the receptive and the active, the inward and the outward, the heart that longs and the spirit that dares.

The Littlest little Princess journeys back to the realm of the Queen, the once-impregnable fortress that had held her power—the palace of illusion, built on control, envy and manipulation. But when she arrives, the Queen is gone. She has not fallen by blade or by war. No, her reign dissolved quietly, like the last breath of a dying star, collapsing on itself.

Princess N, still bound by the chains of sterile wealth, remained in the shadows of this hollow kingdom. She had married thrice—each union an attempt to fill the void left by her mother's envy, each promise a lie unfulfilled. She was draped in the finery of her external successes, but no glittering crown could heal the wound of childhood—a loneliness masked as pride. Her arrogance, like the palace itself, concealed a deep shallow—an appearance of grandeur built over emptiness. Princess N inherited the Queen's legacy but could not escape its curse. She stood amidst the ruins of her mother's reign, and the insatiable hunger for an aliveness she couldn't feel. In the stillness of the palace, the Littlest Princess saw it clearly—the old-world order was always destined to collapse under the weight of its own grandiosity.

Still, a final initiation awaits the Littlest Princess. In the field beyond, an ancient Horse waited—its breath scented with forests and forgotten things. Horses can always find the way home. He asks her: Do you know the trap? And do you know its true name?

The Littlest Princess understood she was made of every name she had earned, every soul she touched. And in that naming, she is freed.

She becomes *Princess Every-Name*—bearer of grief and grace, friend of beasts, retriever of hearts. Daughter of no one, and of everyone. Her name—shimmering with fur and feathers, earth and sky, love given and love received, wounds endured and transformed.

A person who embraces her multiplicity, has lived many lives within one life. Her identity is fluid, spacious and spontaneous—grounded in the living flow of life. The soul, no longer bound by the wounds of the past, belongs to itself, free to be all that it is, grounded in the quiet authority of 'the spirit of the depth.'

The fable moves—as psyche moves—through archetypal landscapes of feminine individuation. Through exile and the devouring mother field, hostile sibling dynamic, flight, encounter with the animal guides, descent into the broken masculine, and the ultimate return to sovereignty. This is the story of the Self—whole, radiant, many-named—emerging from its own forgetting.

The Princess Who Found Her Name ends, as all true stories do, with opening. The final lines are not a boundary, but a threshold.

"Together they sang *Amazing Grace*"—a hymn of redemption.

Amazing grace, how sweet the sound
That saved a soul like me.
I once was lost, but now am found
Was blind, but now I see.

This is the song of the individuated soul—found, gathered, re-membered. Not flawless. But free.

Wild Freedom: A Commentary about Sisters, Minks and Spirituals

By Henry Abramovitch

For my chapter, I want to draw inspiration from beautiful and moving text by one of Israel's most beloved poets, Zelda. It is a poem sung at Israel's Memorial Day events and which most Israelis know by heart:

> Everyone has a name
> given to him by God
> and by his father, his mother...
>
> Everyone has a name
> given to him by the sea
> and by his death.

In this poem, Zelda reminds us of an important but neglected secret. We do not have only one name, such as on our passport or birth certificate, but rather we have many, many names, given to us in many ways. One of our most profound and long-lasting names, is our sibling name: your identity as a sister (or a brother).

A major part of a sibling name is our identity within the birth hierarchy: "First," "sandwich," "baby," and so on. English kinship terms make no necessary reference to birth order. One may say: "She is my older sister," or "I am the youngest sister." Yet in many cultures, the opposite is true. Birth status, such as older sister, younger sister is so ingrained in the psyche and language of these cultures that there is no birth order neutral term for a sister, no escape from sibling hierarchy. This is the case, for example, in the South Indian language Tamil. A speaker must always specify whether one is referring to "akka" as older sister or "tangai" as younger sister. There is no word for just sister, because birth order is an intrinsic aspect of one's identity and status. These roles and responsibilities of each sister are fixed, inescapable, and lifelong. And this is case for the Littlest Princess and Princess N. Their contrasting birth identity defines them and constrains them. While living in the palace, under the emotional domination of the Queen, they cannot escape their sister names. The Littlest Princess's sister-name is the trap she must name and so overcome.

There is another fundamental paradox about siblings. Sisters share the same home and more genes than anyone else. Yet, despite both nature and nurture, research has found that siblings are no more similar than strangers, and often dramatically different. The idea of niches, borrowed from ecology helps explain why sisters and brothers are so different from each other. One metaphor is how rooms in a house are assigned. A firstborn can choose any room. The next child must find a different room and so on. If one is good, the next must be bad; if one sister is studious, the other will be beautiful; if one will be pleaser, the other will be sadistic etc. For Princess N and the Littlest Princess, the contrast is even stronger. They have polarized identities—the nasty, envious elder vs. the submissive, pleasing younger.

In a profound archetypal sense, we all know what a sister (or brother) is supposed to be. The sister archetype is so familiar. Even an only child knows what a real sister is supposed to be: a warm, caring, lifelong companion. This myth of sisters is profound and true, in theory. But the reality of sibling life is sadly very different. The dynamics of envy, conflict, alienation and worse can complicate and corrupt that ideal bond.

Parental favoritism or emotional inequality can leave sibling wounds that may never heal. They may lead to lifelong grudges which explode when a parent needs care or dies. This can lead to an inheritance fight or even sibling alienation. Significantly, almost all of the conflicts in the thirty-three sister/brother stories in the bible result from parental preference which lead to sibling alienation, from Cain and Abel, through Leah and Rachel, and Joseph and his brothers, and beyond. The psychological cost of sibling alienation is that the person is cut off not only from her actual sister, but also from all she represents within in her inner world. A girl cut off from her sister, therefore, lives a life of fragmentation. As a result, dealing with sister wounds is often the key to individuation, as *Wild Freedom* shows so poignantly.

Conceptually, sibling conflict can also be understood from the point of view of Complex Theory. When sisters interact directly with each other, without literal or symbolic interference, I believe the connection is usually friendly even if not always intimate. Siblings learn to work out conflicts by themselves and acquire crucial life skills, such as cooperation, compromise, or taking turns. The worst relations between a brother and sister result when parental complexes are entangled and infiltrate in their relationship. One clear illustration is when a parent intervenes when children are fighting. All brothers and sisters fight as children. That is normal. Significantly, when a parent intervenes, the resulting level of conflict is almost always worse! *Parental intervention is best limited to cases of actual physical harm or bullying.* The parental favouritism will interfere deeply with the possibility for the brothers or sisters to have a relationship on their own disentangled from the parental projections. A similar pattern occurs with the so called "golden child." A golden child is a sibling who has unique talents, gifts, or sensibilities and is admired by parents and indeed the entire extended family. A wise parent will take pains to point out the specialness of each child. However, this is quite rare. Rather, the golden child will light up the eyes and souls of parents with the result that the remaining brothers and sisters will feel in her shadow, producing a host of shadowy emotions, envy, shame, inadequacy and so on. Clearly the Littlest Princess is a golden child with all the attending consequences.

Wild Freedom opens with a mother who loves her firstborn but also envies her. This envy is passed on in what may be called intergenerational transmission of envy. It is a bracing example of Jung's profound insight that before you look for psychopathology in the child, examine if it does not result from the unlived life of the parent. It reminds me of a colleague who suffered a truly dreadful childhood yet went on to become a talented therapist. Nevertheless, she envied her patients because they had something she herself had never had: a caring, nurturing presence. The way the Queen behaves toward each of her daughters, suggests to me a history of serious trauma.

Nothing is said explicitly, but below the surface, it can be palpably felt. Significantly, no king, no father, no masculinity is mentioned or even hinted at. The Queen becomes pregnant, but the progenitor lies outside the story frame. In fairy tale world, the absence of a father would reinforce the maternal symbiosis. The story implies that really from the beginning of her pregnancy and the birth of Princess N, the child's purpose was to fulfil the narcissistic needs of mother, when it is supposed to be the other way around. Symbiosis is natural throughout first year. However, disturbances around symbiosis may linger for a lifetime. Some people never separate from the Great Mother and experience other people as essentially part of themselves and/or expect them to take care of them with no understanding that they ought to give back in return. Others who experience abrupt separation early on are never secure in their object relations and anticipate abandonment while terrified of it. That is the background of how the Queen throws Princess N away when she finds a new, better substitute love object.

> *Time passed and another princess was born. Now it was Princess N's turn to be envious. As the Queen bent to kiss her new baby, Princess N saw a smile lift her mother's lips. It was the very same smile that had been meant for only her. Princess N felt tears burn her eyes and her heart turn to steel. When the Littlest Princess gurgled and cooed, the Queen's smile grew even more radiant. "I too will make my mother smile," thought Princess N, and set about imitating the baby's strange and incomprehensible sounds. But the Queen was not pleased. "Don't be*

> *ridiculous. Act your age," she snapped, holding the precious infant to her breast and shoving Princess N out of her chamber.*

Is this what happened to the Queen herself?

Significantly, none of the characters in the story have a personal name, only the Queen, Princess N and the Littlest Princess. Strikingly, the first-born daughter has an initial, N. I have wondered deeply about this. In the clinical world, it is very common to refer to a patient by their initial. Nevertheless, I find this practice disturbing. To me, it always references Kafka's character Joseph K in *The Trial*, a man on trial without knowing of what he is accused. I pondered why Dale used an initial. I think she did so to give the inner experience of First Princess, that she was not a full person, that part of her was truncated or cut off, that she was more in her role of being a princess and much less as a person in her own right. In fairy tales, being a princess seems wonderful. But in real life, it is often a burden. Such a special status cuts a person off from natural intimacy with non-royals; you are seen too much as daughter of. In fact, this syndrome is so common it has a special name in psychology, specifically PKs. PKs is a shortened form of Preacher's Kids. A PK doesn't have to be an actual preacher's kid, but a child of any one with high moral visibility in the community, like a rabbi, or Jungian analyst. The burden is that any misdeed by the child reflects badly on the status of the parent and so the child feels inwardly constricted and constrained. And that happens when it's a good kid. Princess N and the Littlest Princess are both caught up in PK syndrome, overly dependent on a negative mother complex. Their emotional freedom is cramped by living in a palace, with a mother who is The Queen.

Why is it that in some families with only two daughters, the relationships between sisters are polarized or estranged, while other families with many children exist in harmony? One way to understand this fundamental dichotomy is through the contrast between families that live in a psychology of scarcity (there is not enough love to go around) and those who live in a psychology of surplus (there is more than enough of love to go around). Our royal family lives within a psychology of scarcity, in which there are not enough emotional resources. Everything the littlest sister receives is as at the expense of the eldest, Princess N.

Another way to understand the fairy tale is as on the puer-senex axis, the eternal tension between youth and age, between possibility and experience, between what was and what will be. Envy is natural, expected and a potentially destructive feeling, especially in an atmosphere of scarcity. Yet the Queen is most envious of her daughter's youth and innocence:

> *Once there lived a queen and her daughter, Princess N. The Queen loved her daughter, but she also envied her. She envied the princess her eyes, which had not yet seen sorrow; she envied the princess her laugh, which bubbled forth at the slightest merriment. She even envied the princess her sleep, which was the sleep of animals safe in their lair. But what the Queen envied most was the princess's life, which was just beginning to unfold.*

The Queen is unconscious of the effect of her envy on her children, and there is a hidden hint that this attitude reflects her own traumatic experience which is implied but not stated. The dynamic of a rejected sibling and a chosen sibling reflects the primal sibling wound of the Cain-and-Abel syndrome.

Death is an important character in *Wild Freedom.* Significantly, he is not portrayed as essentially malevolent, like the Grim Reaper, but as acting out envy of the living. *It was Death who whispered to the Queen that she should birth another child. Death being greedy for more souls to snatch.* That is the reason the Queen became pregnant. From Jungian perspective, he resembles an excluded, shadowy part of the personality who wants to reconnect. It is reminiscent of the dream Erich Neumann recounts of a man fleeing some terrifying presence, only to finally turn around and see a hunchback who grabs the dreamer by the throat, and shouts, "I want a share of your life."

As a result, the Littlest Princess is conceived not from love, but in a narcissistic attempt to deny death. Even the somatic memory of her first pregnancy with Princess N during which she felt wonderfully alive did not indicate a desire to care for a baby, but a maneuver to regain vitality for herself. In some important ways, the Littlest Princess resembles a replacement child, conceived to block out the unprocessed grief for a previous child and find life and vitality through the replacing one. The child grows up in the shadow of her dead sister/brother with the result that ghosts inhabit their inner life. There is a positive side to being a replacement child. It is its close association with creativity. Rilke, Jung, Van Gogh, J.M. Barrie, creator of Peter Pan, Harriet Beecher Stowe, author of *Uncle Tom's Cabin* and many others were traumatized replacement children. I would certainly say that is true for the Littlest Princess, who, in becoming Princess Every-Name, fits this creativity profile. But this profile also fits Princess N who out of bitter envy and rejection becomes a dark gothic storyteller who told her sister stories about red-eyed monsters, witches, and murderers. Indeed, dark emotions or trauma can spur great writing. Stephen King, the king of horror, found his best childhood friend beheaded at railroad tracks; King became dissociated, disembodied at first, but from this seedbed came an outpouring of literary works into that land of dread, which we fear, but to which we are also drawn.

In another way Princess N resembles the "glass sibling." This term does not apply to vulnerable or fragile children, but rather to siblings of a chronically ill child, or one with disabilities. They are called glass children because their caregivers are so focused on the sibling with special needs they tend to see straight through them and neglect their needs. Unless addressed, these glass children may have a lasting sense of invisibility and emotional deprivation. Glass brothers or sisters may easily become parentified siblings. They develop empathy and caregiving skills but often also depression. But with awareness of this pattern, parents can prevent the glass sibling syndrome. However, the Queen only encouraged the golden child syndrome, thus wounding both her daughters.

In the West, people expect to go through their life with a single name. Yet in many other cultures, this practice is considered bizarre. Surely, they argue that as your identity changes, then your name should change as well. In these places, name change is natural way to reflect a spiritual or life cycle journey. In these cultures, names are not labels, but deep semiotic indicators of destiny, indicating, as Jung suggested, a person's essence. This is the exciting revelation that transforms the Littlest Princess into Princess Every-Name that concludes *Wild Freedom*. With every name, she can now be whoever she wants to be.

When the Littlest Princess finally returns home, I believe she secretly hoped for a soulful reunion with her older sister, in the spirit of the Vietnamese proverb, "Sisters should be as close as hands and feet." One of life's most unexpected joys is the adult reconciliation with a former sister-enemy. Sisters are guardians of a childhood, as the Spanish author, Clara Luz Zuniga Ortega describes:

> *To the outside world we all grow old. But not to brothers and sisters. We know each other as we always were. We know each other's hearts. We share private family jokes. We remember family feuds and secrets, family griefs and joys. We live outside the touch of time.*

The Brazilian Jungian analyst likewise claims that siblings guard our memories and witness our lives (Barcellos 2015). Sibs are the sole witnesses of our childhood experience. However, in *Wild Freedom* the returning Littlest Princess is completely disappointed. Instead, she finds her old home, abandoned and neglected,

> *the home of spiders and roaches and bats...The palace grounds badly needed tending. Thick-necked weeds and briars choked the gardens. The groomed lawns grew into waist-high meadows...*

It is a poignant image of a neglected center, a neglected home, a neglected Self.

Instead, the Littlest Princess's true home-coming is with the river:

> *Nothing about the river had changed. It was as she had remembered it, a brushstroke of ebony bubbling and rippling over smooth stones. The air smelled of damp moss and the vegetal odor of the water. She looked up. The sky was egg-shell blue with streaks of tangerine where the sun perched.*

Indeed, water holds the tale together from river to ocean and back to river, as the natural symbol of the world of the unconscious, deep and flowing, holding together surface and depth.

I also wondered why Princess N was so unlucky in life and marriage.

> *Princess N had married one, two, three gentleman and since none of them proved worthy according to her standards, she decided to live alone, surrounded by the wealth of her one, two, and three husbands. Rumors spread that she was as miserable as*

ever and blamed anyone in her sight
for her miseries.

One key factor could be the absence of masculine. In her life at the palace, she never broke out to find her own way but rather remained under the impact of the negative mother complex. The absence of masculine presence, leading to negative animus and unconscious wish for her partner to make up for all her deficiencies and losses, a sure recipe for marital disaster and a life without happiness.

Mink

A "mink" in common parlance refers to a lush and showy mink coat worn by a wife or girlfriend given to her by a man of wealth. It is an ostentatious status symbol for the women who wears it, but at the same time indicates her dependence on her husband or sugar daddy. This is the mink that the hunters see in the story:

Mink? a voice exclaimed.
Mink! Mink!! chimed the other. A cape
for my lady.
A blanket for my baby.
Boots for the snow.
A fine cap to show.

Panic spread through the Littlest Princess's body as she listened to the uses the hunters imagined for her pelt. A beauty, she heard one say. Yes, a beauty, came the answer. She's mine. I saw her first. The men began to argue. No, no, the Princess-Mink wanted to yell. It's me, the Littlest Princess, but alas, she could not make herself understood.

The real mink is something entirely different. Solitary. Cunning. And ferocious if attacked. Many traditional cultures use animals as cultural symbols. This symbolism is especially true for Native Americans, where the mink is as a trickster, symbol of transformation with keen, even heightened awareness. It is often seen as a totem animal that represents resourcefulness, secrecy, and the ability to navigate both land and water with ease. In Norse mythology, the mink's agility and stealth were admired, symbolizing cunning and the hidden knowledge required to survive in a world rife with challenges. Another interpretation of the mink in mythology is that of a nocturnal guide or dream walker. Through the physical world the mink can show you how to exist with simple joy and playfulness, but through the realm of dreams he will aid in interpretation and understanding. Minks are known for their adaptability, resourcefulness, stealth and secrecy, playfulness and determination, all the qualities which the Littlest Princess lacks. Therefore, the mink is her perfect spirit guide to help her escape home and is waiting for her upon her return in the form of a horse with whom she shares a joyous homecoming.

Spirituals

During her sea voyages, her bird guide, Hieronymous, sings spirituals as they flew together over the ocean. *River of Jordan is chilly and co-oo-old, Chills the body, but not the so-ou-l...Michael row the boat ashore...It's a-me, it's a-me, it's a-me oh Lord, standing in the need of prayer....Good news, chariot's a-coming, Good news, chariot's a-coming...and I don't want to be left behind...River of Jordan is chilly and cold. Chills the body but not the soul.*

Dale and I share a connection to our shared Jewish heritage, but it was an unexpected joy to see that we also share a passion for these spirituals. Each one of these songs is familiar as old friends from childhood and adolescence when I would sing them with my brother and sister, or at summer camp or even at protests. But I also wondered why Dale had included spirituals. Spirituals, it seems to me, reflect perseverance over adversity, hope of arriving at a better place and above all, spirit.

> *Singing practically keeps me alive when I'm doing a solo, he told her. I will teach you the words, if you like. I will also teach you how to sleep on the wing, how to fish like an expert, how to milk the clouds for a little fresh water—the essentials.*

Jung was the founding father, not only of analytical psychology, but also art therapy and much more. From his creative initiative came dance therapy, music therapy, drama therapy, eco-therapy, cooking therapy and more. Inspired by Hieronymous, I want to propose one more type of therapy, singing therapy. Singing connects a person with their self and singing binds people together who sing in a community of the song, as it did for Princess-Mink and her bird guide. Indeed, one of the best things a person can do to improve their mental health is to join a choir.

Death Name

The last line of Zelda's poem says, *Everyone has a name given to him by the sea and by his death. Wild Freedom* reveals how sea exploring is the royal road to finding heart, naming the trap, and realizing your own true name. But the final name, Zelda says, is given by his death. This line remains evocative and mysterious as good poetry should be. But as an anthropologist, it recalls a widespread practice in which death **does** give a new name to the one who has died. The old life name is forgotten or tabooed as occurs among Australian Aborigines or the emperors of Japan. It is as if to enter the other side, we need a new identity, a new name.

Before and After

The Talmud teaches that we are not to seek what came before, nor what will come after.

But in reading *Wild Freedom,* I cannot help but do so. In my active imagination, I see the spark emerging from Dale's unconscious and her family constellation, like a seed pod bursting into beauty. Everything was there, imminent. And after the story was finished, I imagine Dale shining. Through writing the story, she has liberated herself from all the constraints of her past. All is imminent. All is possible. Her story has set her free.

Endnotes

[1] Author's translation.
[2] Having a good relationship with your sister is the single best predictor of a long and happy life of well being. See Waldinger and Schulz, *The Good Life: Lessons from the World's Longest Scientific Study of Happiness.*
[3] For more on 'sibling niches' and other aspects of sibling psychology, see Abramovitch, *Brothers and Sisters: Myth and Reality.*
[4] See C. Tucker and D. Finklehor, "The state of interventions for sibling conflict and aggression: A systematic review," and J. Obradović, M.J. Sulik, and A. Shaffer, "Learning to let go: Parental over-engagement predicts poorer self-regulation in kindergartners."
[5] E. Neumann, *Depth Psychology and a New Ethic,* p.81.
[6] See K. Schellinski, *Individuation for Adult Replacement Children: Ways of Coming into Being.*
[7] A. Maples, "Recognizing Glass Children," and I. Hanvey, A. Malovic, and E. Ntontis, "Glass Children: The lived experiences of siblings of people with a disability or chronic illness."
[8] Clara Luz Zuniga Ortega, quoted https://www.goodreads.com/quotes/332237-to-the-outside-world-we-all-grow-old-but-not
[9] S. Robens et al., "Effects of Choir Singing on Mental Health: Results of an Online Cross-sectional Study."

References

Abramovitch, Henry. (2025). *Brothers and Sisters: Myth and Reality.* 2nd edition. Asheville, North Carolina: Chiron Publications.

Barcellos, Gustav. (2015). *The Sibling Archetype: The Psychology of Brothers and Sisters and the Meaning of the Horizontal.*

Hanvey, I., A. Malovic, and E. Ntontis. (2022). "Glass Children: The lived experiences of siblings of people with a disability or chronic illness." *Journal of Community & Applied Social Psychology.* 32, 936-948.

Maples, Alicia. (2010). "Recognizing Glass Children." YouTube video, 19:20, from a talk given at TEDx San Antonio on October 16, 2010, posted by "TEDx Talks," December 27, 2010, https://www.youtube.com/watch?v=MSwqo-g2Tbk

Neumann, E. (1990). *Depth Psychology and a New Ethic.* Translated by Eugene Rolfe. Boston: Shambala.

Obradović, J., M.J. Sulik, and A. Shaffer. (2021). "Learning to let go: Parental over-engagement predicts poorer self-regulation in kindergartners." *Journal of Family Psychology.* 35(8):1160-1170.

Ortega, Clara Luz Zuniga (1994). Quoted: https://www.goodreads.com/quotes/332237-to-the-outside-world-we-all-grow-old-but-not

Robens, S., A. Monstadt, A. Hagen, and T. Ostermann. (2024). "Effects of Choir Singing on Mental Health: Results of an Online Cross-sectional Study." *Journal of Voice.* 38(6):1397-1406.

Schellinski, Kristina. (2019). *Individuation for Adult Replacement Children: Ways of Coming into Being.* London & New York: Routledge.

Tucker, C. and D. Finklehor. (2017). "The state of interventions for sibling conflict and aggression: A systematic review." *Trauma, Violence, Abuse.* 18 (4): 396-406.

Waldinger, Robert and Marc Schulz. (2023). *The Good Life: Lessons from the World's Longest Scientific Study of Happiness.* New York: Simon & Schuster.

Writing as Self-Enchantment: Thoughts on Imagination, Mystery, and the Unconscious

By Dale M. Kushner

Once upon a time, far north in a cabin by a giant inland sea, I discovered I was a stranger to myself. Several months earlier, in the winter of a new year, I had returned from a writing retreat to confront a crisis in my life. I had previously embarked upon a reckless and dangerous path. For several years, I had been deaf to the whimpers the soul makes when distressed. The deafness was a clever trick perfected in childhood, but, as I was soon to discover, and as fairy tales illustrate, at our peril do we ignore the warnings of the clever fish, the talking stone, the bird with the golden tongue—wise instincts that caution of disaster.

You might want to know what happened on that rocky path, but the details of that story are not important. It is enough to say I had fallen prey to an enchantment and had been bewitched. Bewitchment has many sources: substances bewitch. Ideologies bewitch. Propaganda, people, their ideas and desires bewitch. The source of my bewitchment need not be named. What is important is that I was engulfed in a personal crisis that left me standing at an unexpected crossroad. Like all intimate relationships, my domestic life harbored a Pandora's Box filled with the unspoken. Now the lid had sprung and out flew the angers, fears, evasions that had long gone unsaid. Anyone who has stood in front of a mirror minus rosy glasses, anyone who has willingly or unwillingly wrestled with knots of entanglement from the past or confronted well-established lacunae in the psyche will know what I'm talking about.

Personal crisis = a grueling reckoning. For many months I wandered in a fog. Had you run into me then, beneath the composed public persona you would have seen the cartoonish face of a dazed woman. The husk of my old self was in shreds. I stood at the edge of a portal peering into the darkness, bereft of language to convey the pulse-beat of my lived life and the alterations in my being. Fear, guilt, sorrow, remorse ambushed me. I was profoundly lonely. Then came the summer. That's when I found myself at a cabin by dazzling lake writing a fairy tale.

I had never written a fairy tale before, had never envisioned writing a fairy tale, and yet the form sprang spontaneously into consciousness as if I were channeling an existence from a previous life. The poet Adrienne Rich says that the world of the tale is above all "the vale of soul-making."[1] I agree. As a poet, I had always kept company with vivid imagery, but now, in the wilderness, an owl's mournful cry accompanied me as I wrote late into the night; I was engaged in something new. I was creating a narrative, a coherent story, a symbolic account of my inner world. Words surfaced from my depths. Characters appeared and demanded my attention. I transcribed what they said as if taking dictation. If previously I'd been bewitched, the process of writing "The Princess Who Found Her Name" released me from that spell. The fairy tale had a life of its own, but it needed me to become manifest. Willingly I surrendered to immersion in self-enchantment.

How clearly I can see this now: the emerging self's intention was to educate me and transform the vessel called Dale. Her modus operandi was storytelling.

*

Some writers claim to have completed their first novel by the age of ten. Others corralled neighborhood kids to act in plays they'd penned or credit an observant teacher for noticing their gifts and shepherding them into the writing life. I fit neither of those categories. Language is my secondary mode of making meaning; the first is images. I think cinematically. I can still recall the dreamlike quality of entering the landscape depicted on the pages of a picture book I read as a child whose title and story are long forgotten. Outside twilight would sift through the leaves. In bed I'd gaze at an illustration of a densely green forest, beyond which a tiny locomotive disappeared into the mouth of a cave at the base of a mountain. The cave's entrance was the blackest black and sent a sublime feeling of wonder and terror up my spine. This is my first memory of awe. Awe orients us to the Beyond and the ineffable but felt presence of mystery; awe discloses our connection to soul.

In searching for clues as to why an original fairy tale arose in me at a time of upheaval, I return to the charmed feeling of suspended time I felt as a child cozied away in bed with a picture book, of leaving one construct of reality, the day reality of a troubled family, to discover a catalyzing new domain where all things were possible, including magic. Including hope. I needed to impose order on the emotional chaos swarming in and around me. How appropriate that when, as an adult I stood on broken ground facing a hard season ahead, my mind sought a childhood comfort in the imagination's self-correcting genius. Imagination does more than invent. It's a faculty that provides, through empathy, through imagining *other*, another way of knowing. Its original Greek meaning is *bring into light*.

I had just entered analysis before going to the cabin and had begun to excavate unexplored aspects of psyche, but I needed the lawlessness of the imagination to configure a foundational inner story. "If we cannot imagine, we cannot foresee," the French philosopher Gaston Bachelard wrote in *The Poetics of Space*, a book that endears itself to many poets.[2] Yes yes yes! The imagination is a wild playmate who grabs our hand and pulls us out the back gate through the meadow and down the ravine beyond our mother's anxious call and our father's protective anger, shouting *Courage!* in our ears.

*

Nabokov believed that dark subjects hold magic. This aligns with Jung's understanding of the potentiality of repressed energies in the shadow. During that summer, shadow aspects, the half-truths and self-deceptions I'd cultivated to keep me unknown to myself flooded into my awareness. To welcome all parts of oneself is good medicine that is bitter to swallow. Those of us who have been shaken free from denial and self-imposed ignorance or have had to reconcile conflicting needs, those who have embraced the role of good girl or boy while dreaming of feral children, runaway dogs or driving cars at uncontrollable speeds will understand. The constructed good girl craves what she avoids: risk and liberation that beckons toward unchartered territory, threatens constricting boundaries and limitations, and collides with the pre-packaged self. But prohibitions do not eliminate the desire for risk and adventure, daring and transgressions. In dreams, in creative works, the imagination shows itself to delight in mischief and mystery. Mystery sends us back into the muddle to tease out more than the facts and more than the psychological truths at play. Mystery is a flirt that tempts with promises of knowing the unknowable, a force field for the curious and a crucible of transformation.

*

At the core of what I am talking about is an intrinsic conflict: the opposing principles of wildness and domesticity. An animal that is domesticated loses its ability to live in the wild and becomes dependent on humans for its survival. Over time, the animal's behavior modifies to be more acceptable to humans. Think dog versus cat, cow versus bear.

No one would have ever called me a wild girl, a tomboy or daredevil, nor was I seductive or impulsive. In grade school, I was quiet and demure. But also, private and sly. If I embodied wildness, and I see now I *did* embody wildness, it took the form of Artemis's little sister, at home in my hide-away under the forsythia bushes with my collection of horse chestnuts, stones and stolen roses—a girl who liked to race the wind.

This description does not suggest conflict, but of course the movement of a soul through the world is rife with conflict that longs to be communicated, just as the opposing parts of self long to be united in wholeness. The incommunicability of our inner lives fights with a desire to connect, to share our stories. So it was with me: the long practice of staying invisible as a child fought with a yearning to be seen. But now, in the earthquake shake-up of that winter, my elemental individuality, the unprocessed needs and desires suppressed by the roles of daughter, wife, and mother had been fully exposed. The earthquake, the blow-out, the cataclysm, perhaps engineered by the Self, established new ground. Beneath the surface, tension had been building; the released energy became the fuel for creativity. Understanding this is both important and necessary.

*

Conflict is an impetus for change, but change disarms and disorients. We wonder, as I did, this path or that? The way is unclear. The trodden path is obedience, the other fork, the soul's sovereignty. The opportunities for choice come thundering into our lives. It takes moxie to disobey authority and convention knowing retribution or punishment will follow. Loyalty to family versus honoring the Self? Snow White, Red Riding Hood, Bluebeard's wives as well as that original sinner, Eve, all disobey out of curiosity and a hunger for knowledge. To fling oneself against accept norms courts rejection, even banishment. In Jewish homes like mine, depending on the severity of the transgression, the "bad seed" child is considered dead and is cut off forever from the family.

The ability to tolerate that ultimate rejection and survive without its source of love and care is a fear that has shaped generations of women, and I am one of them. It is not Eve who is our model for escaping harm, but Scheherazade, who cunningly warded off a death decree by mesmerizing the Sultan with her enchanting tales. Our gestures of rebellion are enacted when no one is paying attention or are coded sleights-of-hand.

Like Scheherazade, a mythic intelligence became my ally. But unlike Scheherazade, a fantasy figure in a fantastic tale who was not a mother, I was bound by traditional roles. Those roles were and are life-giving and life-sustaining but as many women then and now discover, the daimons of creativity demand everything you will give them and more. They wish to be *the* consuming relationship in your life. They want you all to themselves, they implore you to be experimental, to challenge outworn ways of thinking and being. To engage with them requires a tolerance for the unknown, for uncertainty, for disappointment, failure, and even despair. When the instinct to seek, to create, to be a pilgrim in the wilderness ignites and catches fire, the urge to transgress established rules and taboos and explore without limits can be irresistible. Tension arises between the call for safety and security and the call to individuate. Stability, predictability, self-sacrifice, the *thereness* necessary for good parenting and all intimate relationships are qualities that collide with Aphroditian-Dionysian inclinations. I'm reminded of Psyche's mission to retrieve Persephone's beauty box from the underworld in the tale of Psyche and Amor. Crossing the River Styx, Psyche is ordered to ignore the souls clamoring for rescue in her boat. To complete her goddess-given task and be reunited with her lover, Eros, she must resist her empathic maternal impulse to help the drowning souls and continue with her heroic assignment.[3]

The tale of Psyche and Amor is elemental to womanhood in depicting our deep-seated anguish over self-abandonment in service to others. The conflict resists a one-time fix, is always circumstantial and mutable. The Greek myths, perhaps all myths, are shrewd teaching stories but are rarely directly translatable to life as it is. Psyche's quest is archetypal; we are tested daily in our quotidian choices: walk the dog or write the poem. Show up at a friend's birthday party; meditate. Our dreams, however, know exactly who we are. One night during my summer of reclamation at the cabin, I dreamed that a wild-haired girl wearing a dog collar and dragging a leash dashed from nearby bushes, startling my daughters and me. Disgusted by her dishevelment and terrified by the hunger in her eyes, I rushed the children away, warning them not to turn around and look at the raggedy girl. Decades later, the dream's message is obvious, but at the time I woke breathless and shaken to the core.

I am a daughter and I am a mother, a mother of daughters. I respect mothers, I admire mothers and mothering. Life would be unnavigable without maternal care provided by any gender. Becoming a mother was my second fateful metamorphosis, the first being puberty, and as physically transformational—veins, bones, milk—as Daphne becoming a myrtle tree. Much of what I know about love, I learned by being the one whose arms enclosed a weeping child, whose breasts were pillows for a restless sleeper. My own mother was highly unskilled for the job. She, and I, come from a long line of unmothered mothers. These facts have shaped who I am, and the plight of the Littlest Princess.

*

As the Littlest Princess asserted herself and came into being through me, I too was being born, or rather, reborn. Shorn of an old identity, I was the snake without its new skin, the bald chick awaiting feathers. Fairy tales alert us to this nascent vulnerability as the initiating wound foreshadowing trouble to come. A mother dies soon after giving birth leaving her infant to the winds of fate and we shudder with foreknowledge of the challenges that soon will beset the child. During my period of confusion, I was not that motherless baby, nor without protection and care. Who was I? A woman not quite in the middle of her lifetime. A published poet with an MFA and a budding writing career, the mother of two daughters, a devoted wife in a longstanding marriage. I was also a woman alien to herself, in radical denial of the discord within.

Jung befriended and counselled many artists; I count myself among those who consider Jung a ghostly mentor. When he writes that an artist's life can't help but be full of conflicts, a ruthless passion facing off with a need for security, I agree but wonder if he had female as well as male artists in mind. For the divine gift of creative fire, he writes, the artist pays dearly.[4]

"Divine gift" echoes a vestigial trope from nineteenth century Byronic Romanticism—the gifted but tortured hero with his many muses. History offers examples, mostly of men, whose "divine gift" excused egregious perpetration as a necessary adjunct to male inspiration and creativity. Say "Picasso" and we nod our heads. Childless or unwed female artists who have chosen alternative lifestyles are deemed abnormal, or worse, monstrous. But Jung does name a true conflict: the need to escape versus the need to belong—the Littlest Princess's dilemma. Wrestling with the contradiction in our nature is a lesson in discernment: who is calling out directions? The Self or a determined ego?

*

Crisis shakes the shadow loose. Turns us topsy turvy, and if we are lucky, cracks us open. Cataclysms flicker with opportunity. The pieces of my life lay around me, my old way of being, dismantled. Often, I felt mute. This muteness was the silence after a storm, after the wind blows in, trees tumble and the earth shakes; the silence when calm is finally restored. In that silence, my creative spirit found renewed life; a story about an unhappy princess began to form.

After a natural disaster, we rebuild bridges, roads, homes and schools. After a personal disaster, we are rebuilt from inside out.

Winter into spring, spring into early summer, before the trip north, my mind was bereft of symbolic prompts or galvanizing dreams. I was lost, a word that originally meant "perish, destroy" and later came to mean "gone astray." The poet Theodore Roethke wrote, "In a dark time, the eye begins to see."[5] *Begins to see...* But not always, and not immediately. In a dark time, we stumble, bump into walls, sink into apathy. Nothing looks familiar, or safe. Some call it the Bardo, some say the dark night of the soul. Jung called this appointment with Self meeting the spirit of the depths. He left us his *Liber Novus* and *The Red Book* as guides to a confrontation with the unconscious. His story is not my story, is not your story; what archetypes, symbols, images surface to enlighten us will differ, and yet what these encounters share is an animating force that stands in opposition to a frozen spirit.

But the soul is never empty nor is the void a void. At the cabin, the inland sea spoke in sing-song gasps or lulling sighs. Owl, loon, pine and spruce extended their mediating influences. Jung writes about the unlimited knowledge present in nature, comprehended only when consciousness is ready for it. Now the hum and buzz of the natural world welcomed me, and I let it in. The panic in my heart subsided; the fog began to lift. Something was dying off, like the dimming of an aging star losing its light; something was incubating, about to be born. I could not have said this then, but I can say it now: when you stand in the rubble that was once the solid edifice of your life, believing everything precious has been destroyed, take off the blinders. The trees have not stopped their miracle of photosynthesis; the bees are making honey in their castles of wax; a nearby porcupine is shuffling into its den.

I removed my blinders; I saw creation vibrating everywhere, all things touching and relating to other things, whole.

*

I can recount that summer and the all-embracing feeling of refuge the wilderness extended. Minnows flash in the shallows. The bass are spawning, turtles are laying their eggs. Black bears stumble out from their long sleep. I have also been asleep, asleep to myself and have come far north to attend to my shattered self. My husband has come with me, but like so much of my experience that summer, solitude is an inner experience.

Every day I walk the beach along the lake and mull over the questions my analyst has put to me in his gently probing manner. In the analytic chamber, which that summer was a phone booth under a guardian pine, we enter the timeless realm of dream story-time where my mother and sister smolder and vent, accompanied by disjoined memories, cryptic images and scenarios of ominous and intruding dangers. The vulnerable self is not easily lured from her hiding place. Even in a nurturing and safe environment, it is difficult to let go of the props that define the persona.

According to the Law of Similars, like cures like. I needed a new enchantment to banish the prior bewitchment. The first gateway has swung open, and the journey begun. Enter magic.

*

I call my analyst weekly from the outdoor payphone. His voice is ballast. He seeds our conversations with mythic tales and folk stories that amplify an unconscious brew of issues and concerns. Soon I begin to see how my travails are not unique to me but belong to humanity. As Whitman reminds, I contain multitudes. I'm rocked by the power of archetypes. Demeter and Persephone; Rapunzel and her rapacious mother; the girl whose hands grow back. Stories that have captivated audiences over millennia now captivate me. The maidens and their descents enthrall. Innana, Eurydice, Psyche. Even

Alice. I too had been pulled into the underworld, but how to translate the soul's adventures without flattening the experience?

A massive shift, a quietening and slowing down is occurring in me. I watch sunlight move through the trees. Reeds blaze orange at sunset. The doe that stares from behind the birch is my familiar. I let my hair go wild. Beauty softens the call of madness. For the first time, I let myself know myself and be known.

*

Several weeks into the summer I am climbing over a pile of boulders when I hear a voice. *Once upon a time.* I turn an ear to the sky, as if to catch the voice of God.

Onceuponatimeonceuponatime. I listen harder and hear nothing but an adamant wind. The next morning, flush with excitement, I mount the stairs to the loft and write *Once upon a time* on a new legal pad, then wait. I'm used to this process when writing poems, the first line jumping into consciousness, then silence, then another tumbling out of words until whatever in me wants me to know what *it* knows accepts me as a grateful listener. The waiting and the listening are tests of faith against which doubt repeatedly hurls itself.

Once upon a time, there lived a queen with her daughter. My pen flies across the page to catch the rush of words. The process feels different than writing a poem. In recent years, when I'm asked about the difference between writing poetry and writing fiction, I say writing a poem is like lying in a hammock under a starry sky and trying to capture the immensity of the universe—something beyond language— in a handful of words. Writing a novel is like building a house, stage by stage, room by room, at a particular time and in a particular place for specific people. Writing a fairy tale, I would soon find out, is a marriage of those two impulses, the lyric and the narrative.

The following day, I return to my desk and the Littlest Princess willingly continues her tale. She is isolated in a gloomy palace, trapped and unhappy, forlorn and in need. We are entwined; her plight is my plight, both of us clueless about her imminent adventures or how her troubles will resolve. I do not yet comprehend I am the real protagonist of the story.

An audacious mink appears. Soon other characters arrive—a ministerial heron, a thug-like fish. Not to be ignored, the envious mother and sister claim their space. The work of transcribing is effortless, the process of writing, intoxicating. Like a waking dream, the story unfolds without my volition. This is what Jung might have been referring to when he wrote about inaugurating images that communicate what is kept secret from the ego but reveal themselves in dreams and analysis. Every day I wake in anticipation of what will happen next to the princess. I am the writer, but I am also the one surprised.

*

What happens next? This is the question at the heart of narrative, of plot and story. It's what makes us turn the page. Will the witch eat Hansel before Gretel can save him? Will Sleeping Beauty ever wake up? What is the nature of evil? By what means do we save ourselves? How wonderfully provocative are these existential questions embedded in favorite tales. But when I'm writing I am not thinking about existential questions nor am I consciously planting symbols to make a point. The symbols arise and speak on their own terms. I wonder with Jung, "What if there were a living agency beyond our everyday world...a door that opens to the human world from a world beyond."[6] Fairy tales are fantastical.

Realism in fiction is a refinement of the real minus the fantastical, but the real and the fantastic coexist in life.

What will happen next? This is also my *cri de coeur*, the question that encircled my days during my summer of uncertainty. The past was governed by phantoms, questionable assumptions and wrong-headed beliefs. The future looked opaque. What dangers lay ahead? *What will happen next?* As in fairy tales, so in life. We follow the breadcrumbs until they disappear, and we are left stranded in the silent wood. Then what? Unless provoked, do we question what devouring aspect of ourselves has led us astray? What pact with naiveté have we made? How are we both the Beauty asleep in a glass coffin and the hero breaking the glass with an axe? Which archetypal voices speak loudest? Which is our best guide?

Here is another way I've come to think about the process of writing *The Princess Who Found Her Name*: I was receiving a transmission. I was being infused. Something was energizing me—a vital creative force. I was racked with loss and confusion. At the same time, I had started to glow.

*

Glow. The aluminum shimmer the moon throws over the lake, the blood-red eye of the loon. Glow. The phosphorescence of fireflies, jellyfish, fungi, krill. The bioluminescence of lanternfish in the depths of the sea. The goldfinch whose broken yellow body I hold in my hands. My father and I on a woodland path, the cavity at the base of a tree where he tells me Velvela the rabbit lives. The new glow is a warmth, a warming up, an ember in the central core of my being. It cannot be willed, can be lost or submerged but not corrupted.

*

What is a *true* story? What makes a story *the truth*? Confabulation is one way to tell a tale, and as Emily Dickinson advised, best to tell it slant.[7] *The Princess Who Found Her Name* is a confabulation *and* a true story depicted symbolically through archetypal images that represent an individual's psyche as embedded in the collective imagination.

What does writing as self-enchantment mean? It means writing from a place of re-enchantment with the world; it means writing with a mind that has been liberated from its isolation and loneliness and imprisonment in the darker spheres to reenter and engage with life, seeing all particularities through the lens of love. This love is not personal but radiates from us to every entity simply because we are here, alive together.

Would I have become a novelist devoted to writing my first novel over several years if I had not first birthed a fairy tale during the long weeks of that summer? If I had not written the fairy tale, if I had not been in analysis, if I had not been in analysis with my particular analyst would I have been receptive to the influence of dreams and trusted my imagination? To trust the healing images within? Who can say? Perhaps I am writing this essay, laying down the facts to convince you, dear reader, and myself of the unconscious's unfathomable wisdom.

*

As I write, great troubles stalk the land. Violence and cruelty, lying and corruption have become normalized. We are, as a nation, as a collective, and as individuals, in radical disarray. The rise and fall of empires, kings, sultans, moguls and tribes have occurred since the beginning of time, the archetypal dimensions of which are symbolized as ruinous and ruined kingdoms, greedy kings and barren queens recorded in the oral stories that have become our fairy tales. These stories are a living connection between the old order and the new. The ultimate question they and *Wild Freedom* pose is: Who are we and how shall we live? *Who am I and how shall I live?*

*

I have been afraid to write this essay, afraid to reveal parts of myself and my history. I am both the Dale of the essay and an omniscient narrator who stands outside the drama. I would like to think that the latter stance signifies a mature presence, an observer-self, and that the act of writing has been an act of devotion and a form of prayer. Not prayer as petition but prayer as a direct connection to the divine.

Three words form a chant in my head: astonishment, devotion, divine. Astonishment at what is, what is already here awaiting acknowledgement and praise; devotion to holding with compassion the transformative pain that every stab-in-the-heart inaugurates; the divinity of the non-abandoning Self and its gracious intent to make of the fragments a whole.

Endnotes

[1] A. Rich, "Jane Eyre, The Temptations of a Motherless Woman," in *Essential Essays*, pg. 26.

[2] G. Bachelard, *The Poetics of Space*, Introduction VIII, p. xxx.

[3] E. Neumann, *Amor and Psyche.*

[4] C.G. Jung, "The Spirit in Man, Art and Literature," *CW* vol 15.

[5] T. Roethke, "In a Dark Time," in *The Far Field.*

[6] A. Ulanov, *The Psychoid, Soul and Psyche: Piercing Space-Time Barriers.*

[7] See Dickinson, poem 1263.

References

Bachelard, Gaston. (1969). *The Poetics of Space.* Beacon Press.

Dickinson, Emily. (1998). *The Poems of Emily Dickinson*. Reading Edition, poem 1263. The Belknap Press of Harvard University.

Jung, C.G. (1966). "The Spirit in Man, Art, and Literature." *Collected Works,* vol. 15. Princeton University Press.

Le Guin, Ursula. (2016). "The Operating Instructions." *Words Are My Matter: Writings About Life and Books 2000-2016.* Small Beer Press.

Neumann, Erich. (1956). *Amore and Psyche: The Psychic Development of the Feminine: A Commentary on the Tale by Apuleius.* Princeton University Press.

Rich, Adrienne. (2018). Essential Essays: Culture, Politics and the Art of Poetry. Norton *Essential Essays: Culture, Politics and the Art of Poetry*. Norton.

Roethke, Theodore. (1964). "In A Dark Time." *The Far Field*. Doubleday & Co., Inc.

Ulanov, Ann Belford. (2017). *The Psychoid, Soul and Psyche: Piercing Space-Time Barriers*. Daimon Verlag.

About the Author

Dale M. Kushner, MFA, is a novelist, poet, and essayist. Her debut novel, *The Conditions of Love,* published by Grand Central, was nominated for the Texas Library Association Award for Outstanding Adult Fiction. Her new poetry collection ***M*** was honored by Special Mention in the Pushcart Prize 2024. Kushner's widely regarded writings have appeared in *Strange Attractors: Lives Changed by Chance,* University of Massachusetts Press, *Jung's Red Book For Our Time: Searching for Soul Under Postmodern Conditions, Volume 4, Jewish Currents* and elsewhere. Her short fiction and poetry have appeared in numerous literary journals. In 1990, after the fall of the Berlin Wall and the imminent collapse of the Soviet Union, she was invited to participate as one of three writers from the United States in an international writer's conference in the former Yugoslavia on the subject of "The End of the World Order and the New Utopia." Her poetry collection, *Another Kingdom,* was translated into Serbo-Croatian. Ms. Kushner was also one of twelve people in the arts from around the U.S. invited to the Fetzer Institute for their first artists' conference on compassion and forgiveness. *Transcending the Past,* her popular monthly online column for *Psychology Today,* which bridges art, psychology, and science, is informed by her study of Jungian psychology at the C.G. Jung Institute of Zurich. She has recently been filmed for a documentary on dreams called *Between Two Worlds* now in production. Her interview with neuroscientist Daniela Schiller about memory and trauma is featured in the documentary *See Memory,* seen on public television stations in 2025. Ms. Kushner lives with her husband and dog, Maisie, in Madison, Wisconsin. She has just completed her second novel.

About the Contributors

Henry Abramovitch is Founding President and senior training analyst, Israel Institute of Jungian Psychology in Honor of Erich Neumann, Professor Emeritus at Tel Aviv University, Past President of Israel Anthropological Association who studies mourning cross-culturally. His books include *Brothers and Sisters, Why Odysseus Came Home as a Stranger, and* a novel, *Panic Attacks in Pistachio: A Psychological Detective Story.* With Murray Stein, he coauthored plays, including *The Analyst and the Rabbi* and *Speaking of Friends,* available on YouTube.

Kenneth W. James, Ph.D., is a Jungian analyst in private practice in Chicago and the founder and director of The Soulwork Center, which is dedicated to guiding individuals through the process of individuation, drawing on the insights of C.G. Jung and other pioneers in the field of analytical psychology.

Ken earned his Ph.D. from Northwestern University and holds a Diploma in Analytical Psychology from the C.G. Jung Institute of Chicago. His academic journey also led him to study voice at the American Conservatory of Music and music therapy at the Institute for Consciousness and Music in Baltimore. He deepened his interdisciplinary interests with four years of postdoctoral study in theology and scripture at the Catholic Theological Union in Chicago. In addition to his academic pursuits, Ken has taken lay ordination in Zen Buddhism and studied Kabbalah with a Lubavitcher rabbi in Chicago.

A respected educator as well as a practitioner, Ken has led workshops around the world on topics ranging from the relationship between divination and synchronicity to the use of the Tarot as a tool for exploring the unconscious. Throughout his work—whether in his consulting room or the classroom—Ken is recognized for his distinctive ability to integrate Jungian psychology, clinical expertise, and a lifelong appreciation for the numinous.

Dariane Pictet is a Jungian analyst trained at the C.G. Jung Institute in Zürich. She holds a degree in Comparative Religion from Columbia University (Barnard College) and an Advanced Diploma in Existential Psychotherapy from Regent's University, London, where she also served as Visiting Faculty. She is currently a training and supervising analyst at ISAPZURICH and the Guild of Analytical Psychologists (GAP) in London.

She lectures internationally and gives voice to the symbolic life of the psyche through poetry, performance, and teaching. Her recent publications include:

• "She Walks Northward: The Healing of the Heart in Andersen's Snow Queen." *Jung Journal: Culture & Psyche*, Vol. 20 (Feb. 2026)

• "Reflections on Olga." *In Eranos: A Play*, by Murray Stein & Henry Abramovitch (Chiron, 2024)

• "Mirroring Self-Love." *Quadrant*, Vol. 19, C.G. Jung Foundation (2021)

• "Movements of Soul in The Red Book." in *Jung's Red Book for Our Time*, Vol. 1, (Chiron, 2017)

Brooke Shaden is a fine art photographer, motivational speaker, author, and educator who has been working professionally in fine arts since 2010. She specializes in dark, conceptual self-portraiture and works to destigmatize grief through her art and community leadership.

Viviane Silvera is a filmmaker, painter, and speaker whose work explores the intersection of memory, trauma, and healing through visual storytelling. Born in Hong Kong and raised in Brazil, she studied psychology and political science at Tufts University and earned an MFA from the New York Academy of Art. Her acclaimed film *See Memory*, premiered on PBS in spring 2025, visually illustrates how memories form, fragment, and reconnect, drawing on interviews with leading neuroscientists including Nobel Laureate Dr. Eric Kandel and Dr. Daniela Schiller. She is the recipient of a Telly Award for her hand-painted animation and the Award of Excellence in Painting from the Edward Hopper House Museum and Study Center. Silvera's work has been featured by the Bill & Melinda Gates Foundation, Art Basel, and the Friedman Brain Institute, and is supported by the Oliver Sacks Foundation and the NeuroArts Blueprint. She lives and works in New York City, where she continues to create projects that explore the symbolic language of memory and the unconscious.

Murray Stein, Ph.D. was born in Canada and educated in the United States at Yale University (B.A. and M.Div.) and the University of Chicago (Ph.D.). He is a graduate of the C.G. Jung Institute of Zurich (1973) and is presently a Training and Supervising Analyst at the International School of Analytical Psychology Zurich (ISAP-ZURICH). He has been president of the Chicago Society of Jungian Analysts (1980-1985), the International Association for Analytical Psychology (2001-2004) and ISAP-ZURICH (2008-2012). He is the author of *Jung's Treatment of Christianity, Jung's Map of the Soul, Outside Inside and All Around,* and many other books and articles. His newly published *Collected Writings* so far contains ten Volumes. He lives in Switzerland and has a private practice in Zurich and from his home in Goldiwil (Thun).

Acknowledgements

Every book comes into being in its own mysterious way. Many invisible forces act upon the writer before a single word is written. I wish to offer my gratitude to the spirits of the place where the Littlest Princess announced her presence for surely without their patience, determination and tender cajoling there would be no fairy tale or healing into wonderment.

To my great good fortune, I was also joined in this creative endeavor by four esteemed contributors—Murray Stein, Henry Abramovitch, Dariane Pictet and Kenneth W. James—whose eloquent and scholarly commentaries add breadth and depth to the book. I am especially indebted to Murray Stein for his ongoing friendship and companionship in the mystery and whose illuminating understanding of all the realms is central to my own.

Gratitude to artist and filmmaker Viviane Silvera whose magical illustrations make palpable the longings of the human heart. I thank Dr. Steve

Buser, Jennifer Fitzgerald, and the staff at Chiron Publications for their confidence and support and for tending to the minutia of designing a book.

For my dear friend the poet Leslie Ullman who has probably read and commented on everything I have ever written and offered her invaluable Socratic questioning in response, thank you for half a lifetime of intimate conversations; thank you for your keen observations and your abiding faith.

Judith Claire Mitchell, fellow-traveler, novelist/writer extraordinaire. With profound gratitude for your unwavering friendship, your loyal handholding always delivered along with a soupçon of original wit —the light of your insights brightens the pages of this book.

I don't know what I believe about past lives or the probability of an afterlife. I do know I am joyously grateful for companionship and inspiration of dearest friend Mare Chapman, dearest friend and teacher in all matters of soul.

To Bridget Marmion and Rich Kelley for their enduring support, friendship, keen observations and wise advice on being a writer in the world.

With thanks once again to Brooke Shaden for her stunning cover image.

List of Illustrations

Viviane Silvera, Illustrator

Cover Art by Brooke Shaden
https://brookeshaden.com

www.ingramcontent.com/pod-product-compliance
Lightning Source LLC
LaVergne TN
LVHW022045200926
848481LV00003B/791